D.I.Y.

JUSTICE

IN

IRELAND

Prosecuting by Common Informer

The quick and easy (lawful) way to take on tricksters, tyrants, thugs and thieves in the Irish Justice System.

An Integrity Ireland publication

D.I.Y. JUSTICE IN IRELAND:
Prosecuting by Common Informer

1st Edition 2016

ISBN-13: 978-1-906628-73-4

Published by CheckPoint Press, Ireland.

www.checkpointpress.com

CheckPoint
Press

Prosecution by Common Informer under the Petty Sessions (Ireland) Act 1851

YOU can prosecute ANYONE
as long as you have proof
of a criminal offence

You do NOT need
to go to the Gardaí

You do NOT need
a solicitor or a barrister

You approach the judge directly and
explain the facts "in ordinary
language" on a simple form

And best of all, the process is free!

*   *   *

*(So, let's stop moaning and whining about the
awful state of the country. Let's take the initiative and actually DO something about it!)* ☺

DISCLAIMER, ACKNOWLEDGEMENTS & COPYRIGHTS

Disclaimer: This rudimentary handbook has been produced by members of Integrity Ireland as a service to, and for the benefit of other Integrity Ireland Members and supporters in strict accordance with the declared Rules & Guidelines of the Integrity Ireland Community. It does not purport to be 'legal advice' other than in context of assisting untrained members of the public in their dealings with agents or agencies of the State (and/or with affiliates thereof) who are engaged in the misuse or abuse of authority and position - most notably those who operate under the remit of the Irish Justice System, particularly within the Government, An Garda Síochána, the legal profession and in the Irish Courts.

Our gratitude is extended to those who have posted articles and information in the public arena or who have agreed to the use of their quotes in these books. We also acknowledge the selfless and courageous work being done by so many volunteers and activists around the country and beyond. It is in unity of purpose and direction that we will eventually achieve justice.

Whilst all due care has been taken in compiling this handbook to ensure it is accurate at the time of publication, it remains the sole responsibility of the reader-user to ensure the accuracy and/or applicability of the information herein, and that the same is used or applied lawfully and appropriately. Neither Integrity Ireland nor any of its members (other than the individual end user) may be held responsible for the use, misuse, misunderstanding or inaccuracy of the information herein, and it is under this specific condition that this book is made publicly available.

Table of Contents

PLEASE.. READ THIS FIRST

We have all been conditioned to believe that whenever a crime is committed against us that we should report the matter to An Garda Síochána. The Gardaí will then diligently investigate the crime with the intention of arresting and charging the perpetrator. The perpetrator then appears in Court to face the music. This is how we get justice, and this is how 'the bad guys' get their comeuppance - right?

Wrong! The description above is how things are *supposed* to work. But unfortunately, as many victims of crime will testify, our justice system is repeatedly and systematically failing us. Worse than that, it seems that many of those in exalted positions of authority are greatly abusing our trust and in far too many cases are in fact engaged in criminal activity themselves. Whether this be outright criminality such as serious misconduct in public office; of personal acts of fraud and deception; or of unwarranted assaults on members of the public (for example) - or whether more subtle forms of criminality are at work behind the scenes, such as internal conspiracies to cover-up their colleagues' wrongdoing - it is clear that if YOU are the victim of any such official criminality, then you face a *very* difficult uphill battle (to put it mildly) getting anyone in authority to act on your complaints. Because it remains an open secret here in Ireland that if the perpetrators are in any way 'connected' that our justice system is far more likely to throw up a wall of protection and denials around them - than to expose and prosecute them. This is where this little book comes in.

This book details a free and simple legal process whereby you or I can take immediate and effective action against any other person who commits a crime against you. And if that other person happens to be a Garda, a lawyer, an 'Officer of the Court' or a Government Minister - well, all the more reason perhaps to take firm and immediate action - right?

ABOUT THIS BOOK

This book *"D.I.Y. Justice in Ireland"* has been produced as a supplement to the recently published *'Integrity Ireland SOS Guide'* and is for those who are ready to take direct action against rogue authority figures. It comprises some important new materials plus a selection of extracts from the much larger *'SOS Guide'* which was our first attempt to produce essential information and guidelines to help the Irish public negotiate an often convoluted and confusing justice system with some level of understanding.

This book focuses specifically on the little-known but long-established Common Informer legislation and how the ordinary citizen can prosecute others without having to rely on the Gardaí or the Office of the DPP in support. This is the proverbial 'Achilles heel' of a very unjust, justice system.

Both publications are works in progress that were born out of the experiences of various *Integrity Ireland* members who, in some cases, have experienced decades of frustration, abuse and exploitation at the hands of corrupt authorities and errant legal professionals, and who want to ensure that others do not suffer the same experience. This is the core principle that lies at the heart of the *Integrity Ireland* ethos; that in helping others, that ultimately, we also help ourselves.

For legal reasons it needs to be emphasised that we do not claim to be offering 'legal advice' nor are we qualified to do so - other than as a result of the combined experiences of *Integrity Ireland* members who have freely offered to share their often-painful experiences and insights with others. What we *do* claim to be offering here is some intelligible method whereby ordinary members of the public can use the law to hold errant authority figures properly to account - in a quick, easy and cost-effective way but *without* the need to engage with Gardaí, lawyers or other State agencies who, regrettably, have failed the public so often in the recent past.

This book is produced in 5 x 8 pocket-size format for ease of handling and to keep printing costs down, but as a result, we cannot include some of the full-size A4 forms and other notices from the larger *SOS Guide* which will support your Common Informer applications. We have included some scaled-down versions of those forms which hopefully can be enlarged on a standard photocopier. Alternatively, please contact your local I-I branch for assistance, because the more of us that engage in the tactics of direct action - the sooner the authorities will realise that they cannot continue abusing their mandates to serve the people - at least, not without *some* personal consequences. We would ask however, that if you are *not* a fully signed-up member of *Integrity Ireland* who has agreed to abide by our Terms & Guidelines, that you please remove the I-I logo before using those forms. Better still, sign up with us via the *Integrity Ireland* website or via Facebook and gain all of the advantages of full membership.

This book is copyrighted to *CheckPoint Press* and we would ask that if you require further copies that you purchase new copies directly from us so that any modest profits generated can be recycled back into *Integrity Ireland* projects and support. Bulk or wholesale orders can be sourced at 30% discount by emailing 'bookstore@checkpointpress.com'.

Alternatively, you can purchase this book or the *SOS Guide* online from all the major retailers worldwide or by quoting the respective ISBN's and titles to your local bookstore: **978-1-906628-72-7: The Integrity Ireland S.O.S. Guide. 978-1-906628-73-4: D.I.Y. Justice in Ireland.** Discounted copies are available to I-I members and supporters, and to those who attend I-I meetings.

Finally, as you read through this book, please feel free to alert us as to any apparent errors or mistakes, or, feel free to suggest additional materials which can be incorporated into subsequent versions by emailing 'sos@integrityireland.ie'. Original materials will be credited respectively. *STM 2016*

Ten Things You Absolutely Need to Know

1. The Irish justice system is fundamentally flawed, illusory and inconsistent, and is generally 'unfit for purpose'.

2. The publicly-stated aims, goals and objectives of the Dept. of Justice are NOT to be believed or trusted.

3. On the whole, those in senior positions of authority have NOT been promoted on merit, but on their political connections and willingness to protect the status quo.

4. The self-regulated Irish legal profession is rife with malpractice; fraud, perjury, deception, collusion, and the wholesale abuse and exploitation of the Irish public.

5. Justice-related State agencies such as the Chief State Solicitor's Office and the Office of the DPP - as well as other State bodies such as NAMA, GSOC and the Legal Aid Board variously 'share' key personnel, information and resources with a number of private Irish law firms.

6. Rank-and-file Gardaí are poorly trained and resourced, are poorly paid, and are subject to internal intimidation by superiors, to punitive strictures, secretive codes, and difficult and often amoral working conditions.

7. The Courts Service is a private corporation whose objective and priority is to turn a profit.

8. Judges are politically appointed, and cannot be sacked.

9. There is wholesale inconsistency, rule-breaking and unpredictability surrounding activities in our Courts.

10. At present, there is NO truly 'independent' or effective oversight of any of these agencies, and little or no regulation that might prevent repeated wrongdoing on the part of their various officers, agents and employees; and the current Minister for Justice shows no interest in implementing any.

The Supreme Court Ruling

On July 30th 2015, the Supreme Court of Ireland made a seventeen page ruling in a case which was initiated by Common Informer.

* * *

The right to private criminal prosecution was unequivocally endorsed and guaranteed under the current legislation.

* * *

The simple processes and procedures outlined in this book were likewise acknowledged and reinforced.

* * *

At the time of writing therefore, there is no lawful way that anyone in authority can prevent any member of the public from initiating private criminal prosecutions against any other person.

* * *

So, let's make sure that justice, transparency & accountability matters!

INTRODUCTION

It should be clear by now to everyone involved in the *Integrity Ireland* project that by-and-large, Irish State Institutions are wholly unfit for purpose.. unless of course, one accepts that 'the purpose' is to protect the establishment at the expense of the rest of us.

It is perhaps stating the obvious when we note that these institutions—albeit being utterly unfit to serve their mandates to the public—are actually quite efficient at frustrating any efforts in holding rogue authority figures to account. Those who head up these institutions have all the resources of the State at their disposal as well as the services of multiple layers of obedient bureaucrats who are well-versed in the practices of evasiveness, non-accountability, media spin and protecting 'the powers that be' at all costs. In this manner today's generation has inherited a Civil and Public Service which reflects the morality of the current leadership. When that leadership comprises politicians and administrators of the lowest moral character who will not hesitate to lie, cheat or finagle their way to the top—regardless of the damage it is doing to the country—then clearly, these institutions are NOT to be trusted.

Anyone who has had a serious problem with institutions of the State; such as the much-maligned HSE, the Department of Education or An Garda Síochána (for example) quickly runs into a wall of obstructionism, denials and endless deferments designed to frustrate any efforts to get to the truth. We need only look at the decades-long Morris, Moriarty and Mahon Tribunals which cost the Irish taxpayer hundreds of millions in *unvouched* costs and expenses; the shocking Residential Institutions, Magdalene Laundries and symphysiotomy scandals; the protection of paedophile clerics and the systematic denial of justice to their victims; the State-sponsored intimidation and neglect of individual abuse survivors; the targeting, and attempted discrediting of Garda whistleblowers; the ongoing suppression by the Ministry of Justice of hundreds of legitimate complaints of serious Garda wrongdoing; and the farcical banking inquiries – to see how efficiently 'the powers that be' are, when protecting themselves in circumstances that are morally indefensible. This is an alarming situation which should be absolutely unacceptable in a so-called democratic republic, and it remains a matter of bewilderment to many outside professionals that the Irish people continue to put up with this, especially after so much sacrifice in the historical quest for sovereignty and freedom from foreign oppression.

This endemic problem cannot be solved 'from the bottom up' because the problem is NOT in the lower ranks. Most people who enter State institutions are decent, hardworking and sincere at the time they begin their careers – but a system that is controlled by corrupt or compromised authorities cannot but reflect *their* particular skewed 'values' – which in turn demands compliance from subordinates if they are to prosper in that environment. Indeed, trying to maintain one's moral integrity in these compromised conditions only ensures that there will be no meteoric rise to the top for any such earnest souls. *That* overprized experience is reserved for those who understand the dynamics of cronyism, and whose consciences have been dulled by the promise of promotion and of financial reward.

In such a manner, nepotism, bias and clandestine 'favours' done and received have greatly undermined the efficacy and purpose of an overblown public sector whose misguided concept of 'service' is rooted in an abject deference, as demanded by venal superiors. Rooted in a conscience-numbing 'jobs-for-life' culture where 'professional standards' are alarmingly inconsistent and where bonus payments are dished out gratuitously regardless of performance, it is little wonder that even the most junior of officials soon develops an inappropriate sense of cosy entitlement, and comes to see 'service to the public' as a nuisance and a distraction from their *real* day-to-day duties; which is to gratuitously serve and protect their superiors and thus protect their own wages, prospects and pensions. After decades of creeping disregard and contempt for the public, these are the so-called 'values' which underlie practically all of our State institutions. This includes our so-called 'statutory oversight bodies'—the various regulators, ombudsmen, tribunals and 'special review panels'—whose Board members and adjudicators have been cherry-picked from a disturbingly shallow pool of well-connected operators who absolutely *know* which side their bread is buttered. Solemn proclamations by State agencies that these appointments are being made only after a *'robust, impartial and transparent interview process'* are simply not credible - a lie which is exposed with any cursory inspection of the various appointees' background and connections.

The same creeping malaise infests An Garda Síochána where senior management do not 'rise through the ranks' on merit, but instead, gain promotion based upon their political and social affiliations. This causes considerable dismay amongst dedicated ranking Gardaí as well as fuelling public disquiet that our so-called *'Guardians of the Peace'* might occasionally struggle to distinguish who it is they are actually being paid to serve; the people, or a corrupt political establishment? Unfortunately, the same is also generally true of our judicial appointments system which is anything but 'truly independent' or 'transparent' functioning in effect as a gilt-edged platform of reward for compliant legal professionals who are already well-embedded in prevailing political circles. When it comes to positions of trust, power or authority it seems, it's just more of the same old cronyism and nepotism at work—with all of the same old expected outcomes—and the higher we go of course, the greater the perceived risk of ethical and moral contamination.

CORRUPTION, CRONYISM & CRIMINAL COVER-UPS

Nobody is suggesting that corruption doesn't exist in some form or another in every country on earth. However, what makes Ireland somewhat unique when it comes to domestic corruption in the 21st Century, is the breadth and depth of that corruption in such a young and supposedly 'modern' democracy, where so many agencies of the State prioritise (as an undeclared objective) the wholesale exploitation and deception of the public; the cover-up of systemic white-collar and political crime; and the protection of well-connected wrongdoers who profit abundantly, and repeatedly, at our collective expense. But this endemic duplicity didn't become an established—even accepted—part of the socio-political culture overnight. It is the product of the coming-together of a number of elements which, although they may to some extent explain how our 'land of saints and scholars' has fallen so far, does not in any moral sense excuse the behaviour of those involved, nor release us from our collective moral duty to challenge, expose and confront those responsible.

Some of the elements which have contributed to this 'perfect storm' scenario are:

- Ireland's tribal past and the ingrained urge to 'look after' one's friends, relatives and supporters; an under-standable, even admirable ethos - except when it is being done dishonestly. at so many others' cost and expense.

- The 700 years of British rule which set a colonial-style model of oppressive governance which is still being aped - in various ways - by those in positions of power.

- The inheritance of a fully-fledged State infrastructure from the British which was adopted more-or-less wholesale by the fledgling Irish State, but *without* the requisite expertise, experience or checks-and-balances required to function efficiently or truly democratically.

- The evolution of a massively-overblown and wasteful Public Service upon whose good will and support each successive Government depends; the culture of routine pay increases and lifelong entitlement that prevails amongst Civil & Public Service managers in particular; and the prevailing ethos of 'protect the Minister and the establishment at all costs' - regardless of how dismally they may be performing for the public.

- The historical deference of the State and its employees to other institutions or perceived 'authorities' (most notably the Catholic Church, and more recently the bankers, the senior bond holders, international corporations, the EU Troika et al) at the expense of the rights of ordinary Irish citizens.

- The fact that most of the so-called 'statutory oversight bodies' / ombudsmen / tribunals of investigation / review panels or 'official enquiries' in operation today are staffed by 'connected' insiders who have a vested interest in protecting the status quo.

- The prevailing model of 'savage capitalism' which dominates world economies; that advances the inhumane ethos of 'profit at any price'; and which actively rewards those who most efficiently exploit the masses.

The resulting moral and systemic failures in Irish State institutions has been greatly compounded by the greed, arrogance and ruthless ambition of certain political leaders of the recent past and the attitudes of selfish entitlement of their supporters and cronies - many of whom have found themselves being casually promoted to lofty positions of prestige and power for which they were neither technically, nor morally qualified. Arguably, this is what lies at the heart of the problem in the Irish justice system today; too many compromised cronies, and not enough persons of courage and conviction who are willing and able for the task.

This is why *Integrity Ireland* was set up to tackle corruption 'from the top down' especially within An Garda Síochána, the legal profession and the Courts. Because if you *do* have a serious problem with another State institution, agency or individual, you will invariably find yourself dealing with the Gardaí, with lawyers and/or ultimately with the Courts. And if these particular institutions cannot be trusted then we are in a very serious predicament indeed. Because if our law*makers* become the law*breakers* – then arguably, there is no real 'law' anymore, and certainly no real justice for ordinary citizens.

For those of us seeking legitimate relief in 21st Century Ireland, the so-called 'Irish justice system' has become a disturbing oxymoron – a hugely disappointing contradiction-in-terms which exists it seems, only to serve the interests of the favoured few at the great personal expense of the many. It is in effect one great big lie being foisted on a largely-unaware Irish public by well-connected, professional elites whose unworthy interests and ambitions remain dependent upon our ignorance, and upon the longstanding pretence that our legal system and our Courts are in fact something more than the contrived instruments of a so-called 'legal profession'—sponsored chiefly by vested interests—that deals largely in exploitation and profiteering; the collective product of a dark and deceptive propaganda, couched in deliberately obscure language, and wrapped in an oppressive medieval pageantry. Sadly, it has been no great surprise to discover that some of the worst examples of corruption, fraud and malfeasance occur amongst the higher ranks of An Garda Síochána, by State-sponsored 'legal professionals' and by the administrators and adjudicators in our Courts – in close competition of course with some of the more prominent representatives of the established political parties acting in collaboration with the so-called 'privileged elites'. Supposed 'regulation' by their own internal mechanisms - or by insiders acting in the guise of 'independent regulators' is yet another discredited practice set up—again at our great expense—to further deceive and mislead us into believing that someone, somewhere will eventually be held to account.

The *Integrity Ireland* project is not the first attempt to do something about corruption in the Irish justice system, but it is probably fair to say that our recent combined anti-corruption campaigns (with other groups and individuals) have done more to unsettle errant authority figures than any previous efforts by ordinary citizens. Certain strengths and weaknesses in our campaigns are becoming evident as we try out various tactics, and we need to be alert as to what is effective, and what is not. For example, the submission of hundreds of serious complaints of Garda wrongdoing was reluctantly received by the Minister for Justice with a solemn public promise that 'something' would definitely be done about it. That 'something' now appears to be the typical Government response – that of endless denials, delays and deferments (in the guise of a so-called 'Independent Review Mechanism') which is clearly designed to cover up the facts; to protect the wrongdoers, and exhaust complainants' resolve. But now that we are organised as a group and are communicating freely with each other, the usual State tactics of sending out contrived generic 'personal letters' along with convoluted and dismissive referrals to other agencies is simply not cutting the mustard - at least, not any more. No doubt, urgent discussions are afoot in Ministerial Offices as to how to kick this particular can of worms down the road – at least until the next election – when it will of course become someone else's embarrassing problem. After months of hollow excuses, prevarications and delays, it is clear that those who have so very reluctantly 'assumed responsibility' for this mess have absolutely no intention of dealing with matters in an open, honest and forthright manner – not unless they are forced or embarrassed into doing so. And even then, any such 'official response' will no-doubt consist of some last-minute frantic attempt at 'damage control' where the *real* truth will again become the very first casualty. Meanwhile, as per usual in this wayward State of ours, justice for the ordinary citizen goes a-begging.

For compromised State agencies so heavily invested in suppressing evidence of their own wrongdoing the only remaining option is to string us along using all the resources at their disposal hoping that we will eventually tire of the chase. Firstly, they deny any wrongdoing and give us the proverbial run-around. Then, if we persist, they refer us to some other agency or State Department or, more disturbingly, use other indirect 'solutions' such as Garda harassment or intimidation to remind us of our 'proper place'. Finally, if we continue, undeterred, to insist on some *proper* response, they simply go silent – leaving us wondering why our legitimate questions and complaints are being systematically suppressed and ignored? The key it seems is to keep us waiting, indefinitely, heaping delay upon frustrating delay as we vainly hope that 'someone in authority' will actually do the honourable thing. But then we return to the original question; why on earth would they do *that*!? For certainly there is no profit in it – at least not for them. After years and years of fruitless attempts trying to secure openness, transparency and accountability; and after so many ordinary citizens' lives have been ruined by this systemic corruption, craven hypocrisy and lack of any proper accountability – surely we can all agree that it's now time to try something different.

TACKLING ISSUES – BY TACKLING THE INDIVIDUAL TRANSGRESSORS

A man commits a crime. He gets caught. He is prosecuted and sentenced to jail. Everyone understands that he has done wrong. Even he understands that his actions were wrong and he has to pay a penalty. *The bad action needs to have a consequence for the person who acts wrongly.* And that's why civilised societies have justice systems that penalise wrongdoing – otherwise we would have chaos, anarchy and injustice everywhere.

The problem we are facing in Ireland is that many of our authority figures, most noticeably senior Gardaí, lawyers, civil servants & judges are engaging in routine criminal activity and are doing so with apparent impunity. It is a shocking 'Catch 22' situation when the custodians of our justice system are operating in effect as if they were a criminal organisation preying on ordinary citizens and abusing all of their statutory responsibilities. After a lifetime of mundane abuses of the law and the Constitution many of these individuals believe they are above the law – and who can blame them? Whether it be Garda Management, the Office of the DPP, or barristers and solicitors raking in unvouched fees hand-over-first on State projects; or any other number of consultants, State Board appointees or the favoured friends and relatives of senior politicians benefiting from 'insider' deals and appointments; the plain fact of the matter is that the public are getting very poor value indeed from Irish State institutions – and that is putting it mildly.

Unqualified Ministers-of-State and senior civil servants mask their incompetence by hiring expensive self-styled 'consultants' (at the taxpayers' expense of course) whose main area of expertise seems to be finding new ways to fleece an unsuspecting public. Amidst stifled giggles, foreign experts struggle to find the words to describe the rampant incompetence and stupidity on display – not to mention the incoherent arrogance of State agents whose misplaced attitudes of privileged entitlement belong back in the dark ages. The recent voting machines; toll booths; water charges and Eircode fiascos all spring to mind. With all due respect to those who sincerely do their best in difficult circum-stances; one wonders indeed what it costs the country to support legions of inept, arrogant and compromised State employees – who are not only NOT doing their jobs properly in the first place, but who are in many cases doing the very opposite of what they have been paid to do; namely, to serve and protect the Irish public and uphold the the law and the Constitution – and NOT to abjectly promote the corrupt agendas of amoral elites.

As for justice and the administration of justice? Well, there is a relatively simple premise which governs our Irish judicial system. The Constitution *'Bunreacht nah Eireann'* (literally, *'the Basic Law of Ireland'*) is the prevailing legal document that sets out citizens' fundamental rights and how Ireland *should* be governed. The law (as interpreted and applied by the Government and the Courts) is supposed to be a literal, case-specific interpretation of the Constitution. Likewise, judges are supposedly, *'independent in their functions, subject only to the law and the Constitution.'* But what happens when judges for example do NOT abide by the law or the Constitution? What happens when they act in capricious and prejudiced ways? Can they be sacked for incompetence – for making unconstitutional or clearly unjust decisions? The sad answer is no—not at present—not unless two-thirds of the Oireachtas agrees to impeach them; something that hasn't yet happened in modern Ireland despite all the evidence of incompetence, corruption and even criminal activity by certain members of the judiciary.

With all due respect to the *best* of our judges it matters little apparently, that manifestly unjust decisions are being made on a routine basis in our Courts – in direct contravention of our Constitution and of all the principles of natural justice. A recent example was when one of our members *proved* in Court that Gardaí had conspired with the Office of the DPP to falsely arrest and detain him. Having spent many months and several thousand euros defending himself, this individual was rightfully astonished when the judge refused him any compensation whatsoever—not even his travelling expenses—and no-one from the State-sponsored opposition got even a token slap on the wrist. We would later discover that in 2013, the President of the Circuit Court had entered an 'exemption from costs' clause (for Gardaí and the DPP) into Court Rules - something which is clearly unjust and biased, and which creates a platform of immunity for those in the employ of the State who would abuse their privileged positions to visit vexatious prosecutions on innocent citizens.

Other routine examples include Court Hearings being held (illegally) in the absence of Plaintiffs; of Court files and records being improperly interfered with; of routine fraud and perjury going unpunished; of irascible judges barking orders at bewildered lay litigants; of litigants being forcibly removed for simply asserting their right to speak; and of Gardaí blocking the public's entry to supposedly 'public' Courtrooms. To add insult to injury, we then have certain judges overruling each other's legitimate Orders, publicly contradicting each other and sometimes even contradicting their *own* previous rulings and decisions – and all of this is being paid for by us, the gullible taxpayer!

In short; there is very little to inspire confidence in our legal system as it stands. It is in the main unpredictable, inconsistent, chaotic and largely unmanageable – at least for ordinary citizens – who are justifiably losing faith in a so-called 'justice system' where certain judges operate *outside* of their jurisdiction and remit—often personally conflicted—and sometimes even in contravention of the Constitution itself. In this manner inept, errant or wayward judges can undermine and even subvert the Constitution at will – safe in the knowledge that they cannot be sacked, and safe in the knowledge that ultimately 'the system' will protect its own. This unsettling reality was recently demonstrated in the response of the current Minister for Justice upon receipt of a petition containing thousands of signatures requesting the impeachment of a District Court Judge. The petition was contemptuously returned by the

Minister with the absurd and nonsensical declaration; *"I have no role to play in this matter."* This statement was not only a lie, but it was a brazen lie delivered with brass-necked contempt for the law, for the Constitution and for the very people to whom the Minister of Justice owes her position.

So what happened to judges being 'subject to the law and the Constitution' then, and where are the checks and balances in this so-called 'justice system' – a system where 5 out of 6 judges are members of the ruling political party when appointed to the bench – by the Government - and where JAAB (*the Judicial Appointments Advisory Board*) has not held even ONE single judicial interview in over 12 years!? The so-called 'systems and processes' for selecting and appointing judges in Ireland (who are mandated to be *'independent in their functions'*) reeks with political jobbery, insiderism and cronyism and flies directly in the face of international best practice which stipulates as a fundamental principle that there should be NO political interference in the selection or appointment of judges - for very obvious reasons. But here it is an open and accepted practice for the prevailing political powers to assign judicial positions to their own political allies - and far too often to persons who would undoubtedly fail any genuinely 'independent' or 'robust' interview process.

We really have to ask ourselves again; who is being taken for fools here folks? Our judges are supposed to be the very *best* of us. They are supposed to be wise, judicious, fair and independent. They are there to protect us from abuses of the law and the Constitution - *not* to facilitate them. Unfortunately—and with all due respect to those few notable exceptions to this rule—this is exactly what is happening on a daily basis in many of our Courts, and you or I—or any other unsuspecting citizen—could be the next unwitting victim. But there IS something that we can do about this.

TAKING DIRECT ACTION

As we said before, it is pointless trying to tackle this problem from the bottom up, where you face layer after layer of frustrating bureaucracy and will likely never ever get to the real source of the problem. We need to go straight to the top – or at least, go straight to the source. And the source of any given problem is usually someone in authority who is abusing their power and position. The type of 'someone' who *could* effect positive change in the system if they really wanted to. Somehow, we have to convey the message to these people on a very *personal* level that it simply isn't worth the trouble of NOT doing their jobs correctly – and it certainly isn't going to be a pleasant or profitable experience for them if they continue to actively conspire to visit knowing injustices on ordinary, trusting citizens!

You see, the main reason they act like this in the first place is because they profit from it either *directly* (via legal fees / bribes / favours / brown envelopes etc), or *indirectly* through enhanced promotion prospects for example, because it is abundantly clear that the way to the top in compromised institutions is to be ruthlessly efficient at promoting that institution's agenda - which in this case, is to reward the deception, abuse and exploitation of the public, and to punish any efforts at decency and truth (think of the treatment of the Garda whistleblowers). In this manner a whole cabal of career sociopaths have emerged at the top positions in Irish society and governance - and you can bet your bottom dollar that they are NOT going to give up those coveted positions out of any personal sense of shame or guilt. Sociopaths and psychopaths simply don't 'do' guilt. They do greed, self-ishness and exploitation of others, and can do so untroubled by any real sense of empathy for those they are exploiting. These are the predators and the parasites amongst us who can dish out pain, punishment and judgement at will - who can destroy lives and families on a whim - and who, quite simply, just couldn't care less. So…, let's *make* them care!

MAKING OFFICIAL COMPLAINTS

Clearly, passively following *their* rules in submitting official complaints or taking legal action against the State isn't working, and hundreds of I-I members will testify painfully to that. Whether it be the Garda Ombudsman (GSOC); the complaints department at the Law Society; or trying to take a civil action for damages in the Courts, the experience of most is that it is an exercise in pure futility and frustration. Even in those rare cases where a legitimate complainant manages to get an erring State body into Court and is ready to prove culpability in some serious wrongdoing, the State will fight the claim tooth-and-nail to the bitter end regardless of the facts. Then, at the very last moment—and having dragged the complainants through years of unnecessary and often-painful litigation (at the taxpayer's expense)—State agencies enter into secret settlements with the complainants (again, at OUR expense) under the strict condition that those complainants do NOT disclose any of the details - thus ensuring that nobody in authority is ever held properly to account. It is an utterly disgraceful and even perverse scenario when errant authority figures can basically fund their own repeated misconduct at the taxpayers' expense knowing they will never *personally* be held to account for the awful damage and distress they are causing. In this manner, authority figures who have committed some appalling acts of negligence and malfeasance (whilst being paid by us) find themselves in this perennial 'win-win' situation, arrogantly defending their own wrongdoing using all of the resources of the State (at OUR expense again); and then, in the ultimate gesture of contempt, coercing everyone involved into silence by dipping again, into the public purse.

So, what's to be done? Well, it's been shown that expecting 'the system' to hold its own errant administrators properly to account through their own internal processes is, quite frankly, a fool's game and a colossal waste of our time and resources. What is needed is a direct and uncompromising approach by the public that targets individual transgressors in some *effective* way that will seriously get their attention and encourage them to immediately reform on a *personal* level at the very least. For even the Chief Justice herself has publicly stated; *"It is the people who are sovereign and guardians of the Constitution. Judicial independence exists for the benefit of the people.. The concept of the independence of the judge exists to guard the impartiality of the judge, to protect the judge from interference.. The independence of the judiciary is for the benefit of the community, not the judges. It is a duty not a privilege for a judge."* And if this 'serve the community' principle can be said of our judges and our Courts, then the same is obviously doubly-true of more junior agencies of State, where the insidious cultures of insiderism and personal entitlement have flourished on the backs of a largely-unknowing public. This utterly dysfunctional system is populated in the main by compromised State agents who have scant respect for the public and who cannot be trusted to fulfil their mandates in an open, honest and transparent manner. This is in effect a two-tier system of governance which is fundamentally unfair and undemocratic; where an undeclared ethos of deception and exploitation rules, and where those working for the State are essentially exempt from prosecution or punishment.

But the fact is that ALL citizens – including lawyers, Gardaí and Judges – are subject to the law and the Constitution. This leads us to an obvious question: If a Garda were to order another person to commit a crime – is that person obliged to obey that Garda? No, of course not! In fact, not only are we legally required to abide by the law of the land, but according to the *Reporting Obligations* of the *Criminal Justice Act 2011* we are obliged (under pain of serious penalty) to report offences where, *"there is prima facie evidence of the commission of a relevant offence."* In other words, if we know that a particular crime has been committed then technically speaking we *should* immediately report that crime. All the more so perhaps when those committing the offence are the very people entrusted with the administration of justice. This is our first act in defence of our fundamental rights - to report errant authorities _to_ the authorities! It might seem a bit odd at first to be reporting solicitors, senior civil servants and erring Gardaí _to_ the Gardaí, but in circumstances where the respective 'statutory authorities' (the Law Society, the Garda Ombudsman and the Ministry for Justice for example) are actively complicit in covering up serious wrongdoing – and where the Irish Courts simply cannot be trusted to protect our rights in any consistent way – then the law-abiding citizen really has no other choice but to report matters to the Gardaí and have those complaints officially lodged on the Garda PULSE system. At least that way, there is some 'official record' of what is going on that can't (or at least shouldn't) mysteriously 'disappear' and, whether or not there is any subsequent proper investigation by Gardaí or the DPP, at least WE can make reference to these criminal reports when lodging information on the I-I HAFTA Database; when posting on social media or on public forums; when appearing in Court, or, when taking any other actions in defence of our fundamental rights. But the lodging of official complaints with Gardaí is rarely a satisfactory exercise, because other than irritating rogue officials there is little in the way of _real_ public accountability. But there is another specific action that we have uncovered in our ongoing campaign which has the potential to deliver an even more effective remedy in a fast, direct, open and efficient way - and it is the very reason for the publication of the _SOS Guide_ and this book.

PROSECUTING IN YOUR OWN NAME
Although we have had a couple of false starts, and although the system is now actively trying to obstruct us (which they can't do legally - [more about this later]) the recent use of private prosecutions in the District Court by members of the public is proving to be an effective deterrent against abuses

by rogue authorities, and is a facility enshrined in Common Law which should not be underestimated. In the abject failure of the Gardaí and the DPP's Office in prosecuting blatant criminality amongst authority figures, it is refreshing to know that we can take the initiative - at no financial cost to ourselves - to initiate a criminal prosecution in the Courts. As we will show later, the process is free, simple, straight-forward and uncomplicated, and *cannot* be interrupted, prevented or stopped once properly initiated. There are obligations on the judge to follow procedure and if they do not do so, then they are in breach of 165 years of legal precedent and of two recent rulings by the Superior Courts. In short, this process is legitimate and rock-solid, and it only requires of us that we know what we are doing and that we follow a couple of simple rules, and bingo! - YOU can prosecute any other citizen in your own name, and in an open public Courtroom. It is a very new concept for many of these repeat offenders in positions of power and authority to hear they have been summoned to a public Court to answer for their sins and may even face a criminal conviction despite their connections in high places!

Likewise, the simple premise of absolutely refusing to be a party to any activities being engaged in by authority figures which appear to be unlawful or unconstitutional (especially in our Courts) places us back in the moral and constitutional position of authority over rogue agents of the State. As Chief Justice Susan Denham said; *"It is the people who are sovereign and guardians of the Constitution."* So, each and every time you are wronged by an authority figure, you take direct action. You don't just sit and moan about the situation – you take action! You lodge a formal complaint with the *head* of their institution (not their line manager); you also lodge a criminal complaint with An Garda Síochána and send a copy to the Garda Commissioner; you also take action in the District Court using the Common Informer process and, if appropriate, you also bill the individual for wasting

YOUR precious time. We can't guarantee that you will get full satisfaction every time, but we *can* guarantee that you will get their immediate attention and fire a serious warning shot over the bows – and that in itself is a big step forwards.

This has become a key strategy in our battle against endemic corruption, criminality and cover-ups by State agents; to tackle each and every instance of injustice visited upon our members, and target the individual transgressors with the full weight of the law, with the Articles of the Constitution and with the rules and regulations of the institution where they are employed. Exposure on social media is another tool that should not be underestimated, because it builds another public record. Whatever their rank or position, and whatever their own perceived sense of importance, the fact of the matter is that ALL Irish citizens are subject to the law and the Constitution – and clearly, some of these individuals need to be reminded of this quite urgently. No-one likes hearing that a public, criminal complaint has been lodged against them – especially those with an inflated sense of their own importance and perceived immunity from account-ability – and maybe, just maybe, the knowledge that we are ready and willing to challenge and expose serious wrong-doing by senior authority figures, will help to draw their attention to their own solemnly-sworn obligations and responsibilities, and perhaps encourage them to be a touch more diligent and conscientious in their approach to their work? Alternatively, erring authorities face the prospect of public exposure and embarrassment as we publish the various complaints that have been lodged against them, and pursue with a relentless determination, our absolute fundamental right to justice.

There are seven main ways we intend to achieve this:

- By gathering information for the I-I database so that individual I-I members and supporters will be better informed as to the histories of erring authority figures.

- By putting I-I members in personal contact with the victims of rogue authorities for the purposes of direct moral support and to provide first-hand witnesses in any subsequent legal actions or formal complaints.

- To lodge formal written criminal complaints with Garda HQ and the respective authorities 'for the record'; and by publicly naming-and-shaming those authority figures who seriously breach the law or the Constitution, or who routinely abuse their positions in contravention of their respective Oaths of Office.

- By initiating criminal proceedings in our own names in the District Court, thus sidestepping the need to engage with ineffective State agencies and supposed 'statutory oversight bodies' and thereby raising the prospect of criminal convictions being delivered on rogue authorities.

- By refusing, absolutely, to knowingly comply with - or be a party to - unlawful, criminal or unconstitutional activity - especially when instigated by the authorities.

- By billing rogue authority figures for the time, costs and stresses visited upon us, and if they don't pay, by lodging small claims actions against them in the Courts.

- By maintaining our own unity, integrity and determination of purpose - thereby counteracting the unjust imbalances within 'the system' and promoting a genuine cultural change in the attitudes, morals and ethics of the public sector.

In addition to other anti-corruption tactics such as attendance at Court Hearings, making citizens' arrests, and the daring use of social media; this is how we hope to ensure more openness, transparency and accountability in Irish institutions and less routine injustice – by working together in *personally* confronting corruption, cronyism and criminal cover-ups in direct and courageous ways, and by ensuring that those responsible cannot continue to act with impunity and contempt for the public, for the law, and for our hard-won Constitution. A solemn Constitution to which they are each duty-bound, under oath, to protect, uphold and respect.

This modest publication, and the *Integrity Ireland* movement does NOT comprise, *"..a wholesale, collateral attack on the establishment..."* as has been stated in the mainstream media. Nor are we criticising the sincere efforts of those within the establishment who endeavour to maintain their personal integrity in morally-challenging circumstances. No, this book is just a modest attempt to empower ordinary citizens to stand up against abuse and oppression - especially when that oppression is clearly unjust, immoral, and unlawful - and arguably, also criminal.

It *IS* absolutely true to say however, that the *Integrity Ireland* movement is a direct and definitive 'attack' (per se) on the rampant *corruption* and malfeasance that exists within the Irish establishment today - and we will be making absolutely no apologies for that. Indeed, if any particular individual, agency or institution named in this book feels that they have been unjustly maligned or defamed in this publication (and notwithstanding our sincere undertakings to correct any factual errors herein) then that party should of course immediately issue legal proceedings or take the appropriate action 'in the overall interests of truth, justice and transparency' and we will gladly and willingly respond by producing the evidence and witnesses in support of our position in the open forum of OUR public Courts.

If you want to hear more about how we can help you, and how you can help others, please consider joining us at www.integrityireland.ie because..

"One by one – together – we CAN make a difference!"

Prosecuting by Common Informer - An Overview

(Abridged, from various sources as indicated)

Any member of the public, acting as a **'common informer'** can go directly to the Court to take a prosecution. The **common informer** acting as a prosecutor must present evidence which is admissible, legally obtained and not hearsay. Tribunal proceedings or reports are not admissible in any prosecutions. A summary offence is a minor offence, triable in the District Court with the judge acting as judge and jury and a maximum penalty of two years in jail or a €5,000 fine. A summary offence may be prosecuted by a **common informer** provided there is no statutory provision to the contrary. They may of course also be prosecuted by the Garda, aided by the DPP. **The DPP has no power to intervene in summary proceedings to force the withdrawal of a prosecution brought by a common informer.** An indictable offence is a more serious offence, triable in the Circuit or Central Criminal Court with a jury and no limit on penalty. An indictable offence may only be prosecuted by the DPP. **A common informer** can pursue indictable proceedings in the early stages up to the order for return for trial but the DPP alone can pursue it from then to a verdict.

(Village Magazine, Feb 2013)

*   *   *

At common law, any private individual capable of giving information about the commission of an offence, such as the victim of that offence, could prosecute as a **'common informer'**. This right to pursue a private prosecution remains, but **common informer**s are no longer competent to prosecute charges on indictment.* In practice, few victims mount private prosecutions through the District Courts despite their entitlement to do so.

* Section 9(1) of the Criminal Justice (Administration) Act 1924 abolished the right of **common informers** to prosecute cases on indictment. See further Walsh (2002) at pp.592-4.

(Trinity College Law School, 2007)

*   *   *

No single body or person has a monopoly in the prosecution of criminal offences in Ireland. At common law any person (known as a **common informer**) is competent to initiate and conduct a criminal prosecution. This broad competence is now confined to minor offences which are tried summarily (Criminal Justice (Administration) Act, 1924, Sect. 9). For offences which will be tried by judge and jury (more serious offences) the **common informer** can still initiate the prosecution and maintain it up to the point where the defendant is sent for trial by judge and jury (State (Ennis) v Farrell, 1966, IR 107). At this point the prosecution will either be taken over by the public prosecutor or it will fall. Prosecutorial powers also vest in several statutory bodies... Like the **common informer** these bodies are confined to summary prosecutions. Where a statutory body fails to take a prosecution in any case which is within its remit the public prosecutor can step in and initiate the prosecution (Attorney General v Healy, 1928, IR 460).

(From a Report by Rita Cahill)

*   *   *

The common law recognises the right of the **common informer** to prosecute summary offences. A **common informer** is a member of the public and cannot be a body corporate (GAA v Windle Unreported, Supreme Court June 22, 1993). A **common informer** can, however, be a person who is not an eye-witness. In McCormack v Carroll (1910) 45 ILTR 7, Pallas LCB held that a fishery inspector who was not an eye-witness could act as a **common informer**. In a modern context, there are many statutory bodies (such as local authorities, the HSE and the ODCE) which are given a specific right to prosecute certain offences summarily by the legislature. **Previously a garda prosecuting a summary offence** without the fiat of the DPP **would do so as a common informer** (see DPP v Roddy [1977] IR 177). **This would appear to have been brought to an end by Section 8 of the Garda Síochána Act 2005.**

(James B Dwyer B.L., 2007)

* * *

The Garda Síochána Act 2005 - Section 8

(Gardaí can NOT use the C.I. Procedure to prosecute)

8.— (1) **No member of the Garda Síochána in the course of his or her official duties may institute a prosecution except as provided under this section.**

(2) Subject to subsection (3), any member of the Garda Síochána may institute and conduct prosecutions in a court of summary jurisdiction, but **only in the name of the Director of Public Prosecutions**.

(3) In deciding whether to institute and in instituting or conducting a prosecution, a member of the Garda Síochána shall comply with any applicable direction (whether of a general or specific nature) given by the Director of Public Prosecutions under subsection (4).

(4) The Director of Public Prosecutions may give, vary or rescind directions concerning the institution and conduct of prosecutions by members of the Garda Síochána.

(5) Directions under subsection (4) may be of a general or specific nature and may, among other things, prohibit members of the Garda Síochána from—

(a) instituting or conducting prosecutions of specified types of offences or in specified circumstances, or

(b) conducting prosecutions beyond a specified stage of the proceedings.

(6) If a prosecution is instituted or conducted by a member of the Garda Síochána in the name of the Director of Public Prosecutions—

(a) the member is presumed, unless the contrary is proved, to have complied with this section and any applicable direction given by the Director under this section, and

(b) nothing done by the member in instituting or conducting the prosecution is invalid by reason only of the member's failure to comply with this section or that direction.

(7) **Nothing in this section—**

(a) precludes the Director of Public Prosecutions from, at any stage of the proceedings, assuming the conduct of a prosecution instituted by a member of the Garda Síochána, or

(b) **authorises a member of the Garda Síochána to institute a proceeding without the consent of the Director of Public Prosecutions if an enactment prohibits the institution of that proceeding except by or with the Director's consent.**

(8) For the purpose of this section—

(a) a direction is of a general nature if it relates to a class of prosecutions, and

(b) a direction is of a specific nature if it relates to the prosecution of a person for a specific offence

In short - Gardaí can NOT use the Common Informer process to prosecute us. But they CAN be prosecuted BY us - as can any other Irish citizen - of whatever rank.

Other Important Stuff That You Need to Know

Civil or Criminal - Summary or Indictable Offence?

The Common Informer process is only used to prosecute *criminal* offences (as opposed to civil claims) in the Courts. If a *civil* case is taken against you and you lose the case, then you may have to pay personal damages - and/or obey Court Orders. You can NOT be sent to jail. But if a *criminal* case is taken against you and you lose, then you CAN go to jail and/or receive a fine payable to the State.

There are basically two types of criminal offence in Ireland, namely 'summary' and 'indictable' offences - and it is vitally important that we know the difference between the two.

'Summary' means 'minor'. It is a lesser offence which carries smaller penalties for the offender.

'Indictable' means a more serious offence which carries heavier fines and longer terms of imprisonment.

Some crimes (such as assault, or fraud) can be either 'summary' or 'indictable' depending on the gravity of the offence and/or the injury or loss suffered by the victim.

One judge acting alone can deal with summary offences, but you must have a judge and a jury to deal with indictable offences. (There are some exceptions to this rule - but for the sake of clarity and simplicity let's stick with the basics).

Usually, one-judge criminal cases are heard in the District Court, and judge-and-jury cases are heard in the Circuit Courts or the High Court, but all Common Informer applications *must* begin before a District Court Judge. In short, we must *initiate* both processes in the District Court.

When we initiate a private criminal prosecution in our own names under the Common Informer rules, then we can only maintain control (or 'jurisdiction') over the prosecution of that case as long as it remains a summary (or minor) offence.

If the allegation we are making constitutes an indictable offence, then the Office of the DPP will take over the case and either prosecute - or not - as they see fit. So if we want to maintain jurisdiction and control of the case from start to finish, then the offence must remain a summary one.

Generally speaking, summary offences will attract a prison term of less than 12 months, or a fine (depending on the class of offence) as follows. Class A (up to) €5,000; B, €4,500; C, €2,500; D, €1,000 & E, €500.

To summarise; any citizen can *initiate* a criminal prosecution in the District Court by using the *Common Informer* legislation based on the *Petty Sessions (Ireland) Act 1851*. But if the Court decides that the offence is NOT a summary offence, but must be tried on indictment, then the case has to be heard in a higher Court before a judge and jury. If this happens, then jurisdiction for the continuation and prosecution of the case is passed to the Office of the DPP (the Director of Public Prosecutions) and they take over the case.

Now this would be all well and good if the Office of the DPP was staffed by genuinely 'independent' and diligent professionals who prosecuted crimes in the name of the people according to the principles of natural justice. But again, there appears to be a major problem in the way that the Office of the DPP does business, with an abject failure to prosecute 'connected' or white-collar criminals - while on the other hand demonstrating a reckless enthusiasm in targeting motorists, activists, public protestors and various other minor offenders.

In the circumstances, it is a very handy 'get out of jail free' card for rogue authority figures - knowing that they can only be prosecuted privately by ordinary citizens at the *summary* (minor offence) level where they face only *one* judge and very limited consequences - and if things get too serious then the matter will be passed to the DPP who can then decide - (without explaining the decision to *anyone* believe it or not) - whether or not to continue the prosecution at the *indictable* (major offence) level. This is why is is important that we understand the difference between summary and indictable offences, because if we really do want to have our day in Court - safe from interference from the State - then we have to present our case, and maintain the case, at the summary level in the District Court.

Alternatively, we can *initiate* proceedings in the District Court for indictable (more serious) offences, but we will then have to accept that jurisdiction will be passed to the State, along with the high likelihood that the wagons will be circled to protect the accused - as per usual. But all is not lost, because European legislation came into effect in November 2015 which obliges the DPP to give *some* explanation for often-unfathomable decisions. And if you or I are the party that initiates the criminal complaint in the District Court, then at least we will have a direct personal interest in the case, and can lobby/pursue/question the DPP about any developments or decisions made.

Finally, although there is a statutory time limit of 6 months within which a summary offence has to be prosecuted, *Section 7.4 of the Criminal Justice Act 1951* exempts indictable offences from any such time limits. In other words, if you have evidence of serious wrongdoing then there is NO time limit for taking private prosecutions.

So, let's form an orderly queue, shall we?

Jurisdiction: Summary & Indictable Offences

	Summary	Indictable
Time limit	6 months	None
Prosecutor	Member of public	Office of DPP
Before	One Judge	Judge & Jury
Court	District Court only	District, then Circuit or High Court

This chart shows the general rule. There are some exceptions which should not usually concern us if we are prosecuting by Common Informer at the summary level. However, if for example we initiated an indictable offence and the matter was then passed to the DPP and the accused pleaded guilty - then the DPP can offer the accused the option of being tried by one Judge in the District Court where the penalties are not as severe. This option is ostensibly to save on the costs, time and trouble of organising a Judge-and-jury trial which becomes largely unnecessary if the accused is pleading guilty.

However, it is also a handy option of course, for privileged or connected persons who are facing undeniable criminal charges, to chose a softer option. This is one leading reason why we are probably better off only lodging summary prosecutions - and keeping them at that level - because then WE can maintain control of the prosecution all the way.

Typical Offences Committed by Authority Figures

A full list of the Irish Crime Classification System (ICCS) can be found online or in Part 1 of the I-I SOS Guide.

Assault

Breach of Court Orders

Breach of the Peace

Concealment of Crime

Collusion * Conspiracy * Corruption

Criminal Damage * Contempt of Court

Deception

Failing to Respect Court Summons

False Imprisonment

Forgery * Fraud

Harassment * Intimidation

Misconduct in Public Office

Obstructing the Administration of Justice

Obtaining by False Pretences

Perjury

Personal Injuries

Perverting the Course of Justice

Public Mischief

Robbery

Theft * Trespass

For a list of the specific Act, Law or Statute which has been breached (which you WILL need to advance your case) please visit http://www.irishstatutebook.ie/ online.

The Supreme Court & High Court Rulings

A summary of key points and arguments, by Stephen T Manning

In a 17-page Judgment delivered by the Irish Supreme Court on 30ᵗʰ July 2015 and authored by Mr Justice Clarke [S C Appeal No: 402/2013] the absolute right of private prosecution under the 'Common Informer' legislation was upheld as per the following verbatim quotes thereof.

- **Text in bold** in this section represents OUR questions.

- *Text in italics* represents verbatim quotes from the Supreme Court judgement.

- Normal text is commentary by STM.

---

*   *   *

Q 1: Whether the right to private prosecution had been abolished or was no longer 'legally possible'?

Para 2.1: *"..no express provision is to be found in that legislation terminating the private prosecution of criminal offences."*

Para 4.1: *"Since 1986, two parallel systems for the issue of summonses in criminal matters have co-existed in Irish law. The first system ... is the common informer system under the 1851 Act."* This requires 'consideration' by a District Court Judge before the case can proceed - as described in this book.

The second system is that under which 'authorised persons' (such as the DPP, Attorney General or Gardaí etc) can issue routine summonses <u>without</u> the *prior* consideration of a Judge, whereby the matter is then dealt with in Court.

Para 7.2: The DPP, Justice Hogan, District Court Judge Ryan and the Supreme Court [Denham C.J. / Hardiman J. / O'Donnell J. / Clarke J. / Dunne J.] all agree that, *"it would require clear wording in relevant legislation to establish* *that a long existing legal entitlement to maintain a private criminal prosecution had been abolished."*

*   *   *

Q 2: Regarding whether it can even be <u>implied</u> that the right for Common Informer prosecutions for indictable offences has been abolished?

Para 7.3: *"In my view, such an implication is not permissible."*

*   *   *

Q 3: Regarding any supposed pre-requisite to preview any Common Informer application (by Courts Service Staff etc) so as to avoid any unfounded or vexatious applications?

Para 7.3: *"..the requirement that the common informer satisfy a District Court Judge that it is appropriate to issue a summons provides an adequate safeguard."*

Therefore, it is NOT necessary nor is it historical practice (as has been suggested by certain Courts Service Staff) to have paperwork 'previewed' before presentation to the Judge.

*   *   *

Q 4: To the question of whether the Oireachtas intended to abolish the Common Informer system so far as <u>indictable</u> offences are concerned?

Para 7.4: *"In my view, no such implication can or should be drawn. I would therefore uphold the finding of the trial Judge that the common informer system continues to subsist."*

Para 4.2: *"In the State (Ennis) v. Farrell [1966] I.R. 107, this Court held that a private individual may conduct a prosecution in respect of an indictable offence* (which is) *not triable summarily, up to the return for trial."* (Brackets and punctuation added for clarity)

Please note the clear reference to 'indictable' (more serious) offences and the obvious implication that the using of the Common Informer system to prosecute summary (less serious) offences is therefore doubly asserted.

*   *   *

In a previous ruling in the High Court delivered on July 9th 2013, Justice Gerald Hogan said:

"The right of private prosecution has not been indirectly affected by the abolition of the preliminary examination procedure by the Criminal Justice Act 1999. In the light of The State (Ennis) v. Farrell, clear and express statutory language would be required for this purpose. The special and varying definitions of the word "prosecutor" now contained in s. 4 of the 1967 Act (as inserted by s. 8 of the 1999 Act) **provides clear indication that the Oireachtas, so far from evincing an intention to abolish the right of private prosecution, actually intended to preserve it.**"

*   *   *

In other words:

1. That the public's right to initiate private prosecutions via the Common Informer process is absolutely rock-solid.

2. That there is no need or requirement for any pre-checks or other obstructive qualifiers before presenting one's evidence directly to the Judge in the District Court.

3. That any attempts by Officers of the Court to obstruct or delay these applications would most likely be unlawful.

4. That there is NO excuse in law (or otherwise) for us NOT to bring these private criminal prosecutions asap!

5. So.......? What are we waiting for?

The Authority to Prosecute

In *People (D.P.P.) v Roddy [1977]*, the Supreme Court held that a prosecution may be brought by a member of the Garda Síochána 'in the name of the DPP' without getting the DPP's specific authorisation.

Prior to the Criminal Justice (Amendment) Act, 1924, police officers prosecuted in their own names as members of the public acting as **common informers**. In *Wedick v. Osmond & Son Ltd., [1935]* **it was held that the words "person (official or unofficial) authorised in that behalf by the law for the time being in force" contained in section 9(2) of the Act of 1924 included a common informer, and that his right to prosecute was preserved by that section.**

In *State (Cronin) v Circuit Court Judge of the Western Circuit [1937]*; it was stated (per Kennedy C.J.) that **"where no statute debars an officer of the Garda Síochána, or any other person, in the guise of a common informer, such person is entitled to lay a charge before the District Justice in the first instance".**

There are a number of statutes which specifically prohibit the initiation or the continuance of a prosecution without the specific sanction of the Director of Public Prosecutions and compliance with this prerequisite is necessary to validate the relevant prosecution.

Numerous statutes provide that specific offences may be prosecuted by designated persons, statutory bodies, Ministers of State etc. In *Courtney v Well Woman Centre Ltd.*, the High Court held that the conferring of power on a particular body to prosecute any particular offence does not exclude a member of the Garda Síochána from prosecuting such offence unless there is a clear expression of exclusion of his authority to do so.

In *State (Collins) v Ruane [1985]*, the Supreme Court held that **the Director of Public Prosecutions has NO power**

to compel the withdrawal of a complaint made by a common informer.

In *Dillane v. Attorney General and Ireland [1980]*, the Supreme Court held that a member of the Garda Síochána who prosecutes as a common informer acting in the discharge of his duties as a police officer is entitled to the exemption from costs provided for by Order 36 of the District Court Rules, 1997.

However, *Section 8 of the Garda Síochána Act 2005* has now removed the right of prosecution by Common Informer by members of An Garda Síochána.

Please also see pp. 40-52 of the *Integrity Ireland SOS Guide* ISBN: 978-1-906628-72-7

"Legitimacy, Fairness and Credibility within the Criminal Justice System"

"In order to have ongoing public support and trust, criminal justice systems need to operate in a rule-based and accountable fashion. Arbitrary, corrupt or oppressive measures will ultimately undermine the authority and credibility of the system and, in turn, the rule of law generally. The Irish criminal justice system is founded on Constitutional and common law principles of fairness and respect for individual liberty, and, in particular, the right to a fair trial and a presumption of innocence. It is also essential, however, in the interests of efficiency and in order to instil public confidence, that the system functions effectively and protects the public."

From the Irish Government white paper on Crime, 2011

Tricks & Deception, Delays & Obstruction

During the past few months, we have approached several District Courts with the intention of lodging Common Informer applications. With the exception of the very first application (where it seems we took them by surprise) the authorities have since engaged in a broad range of obstructive, delaying and preventative measures which are clearly and obviously designed to stop us using this process to prosecute serial wrongdoers in the pay of the State.

The problem they are facing however, is that they can NOT _legitimately_ stop us using this process - so they are doing so illegitimately, using various forms of obstruction, deception, misinformation, evasiveness, inventing new procedures, introducing new fees and charges, avoiding personal summonses, and generally breaking all of their own long-established rules and regulations in a desperate attempt to avoid being held accountable under the law for criminal acts.

From our point of view, the interesting thing is that the authorities are more-or-less trapped by the Supreme Court ruling (on the previous pages) into honouring any legitimate request for summonses under this legislation. But this hasn't stopped a number of Judges, Registrars, State-sponsored lawyers and Courts Service Staff from pulling all sorts of ploys, trickery and deception, and generating long delays and obfuscation, in their increasingly farcical efforts to stop us. And the more of this they try to do - and the more it is seen by the public - the quicker the Irish people will come to realize that our so-called justice system - and many of those employed in it - are utterly unfit for purpose.

These are some of those incidents, and this is what you have to look out for when you try to process your applications.

A. Courts Service Staff saying you have to lodge the paperwork with them first. Not true. The legislation is quite specific about the fact that we can approach the judge directly. The Courts Service have used this excuse a few times to prevent applications being heard by the judge, but they are going against 165 years of precedent, against the legislation, and against the Superior Court rulings. On one occasion after we DID lodge our paperwork with them beforehand, they wrote back to us saying that they had discussed the matter with the judge in private and she had directed them to write to us explaining that she had no jurisdiction to hear the applications. It is NOT the Courts Service's job to discuss your case with the judge. It is yours! So, not only was the stated position of the judge very dubious - but both the judge and the Courts Service were basically 'making up the rules' as they went along. They can't do this.

B. Judges saying they can make up new rules at will. No they can't. On one occasion after a judge walked out of Court without dealing with us, we told the Clerk we were going to make a complaint to the European Court of Human Rights, whereupon we were invited into a private meeting with that judge - who then tried to convince us that she had the right to introduce new procedures supposedly 'for the efficient running of the Court'. We told her that she was breaking 165 years of precedent and Superior Court rulings, and therefore we could NOT accept what she was saying or doing.

C. Judges running away. Yes, I know it's hard to believe, but this has happened on a number of occasions in District Courts in Castlebar, Ballina, Roscommon and Dublin in the past few months - even after we had informed the Court Clerk that we were waiting to lodge applications. Now, when we say 'running' we really mean 'exiting in haste', but in some instances the judge has definitely surrendered their personal dignity in their hurry to get out of the Courtroom.

On one or two occasions we were actually in the process of verbally informing the Judge that we had Common Informer applications to process, but at the mention of the 'C.I.'

words, some sort of internal flight mechanism seemed to kick in and the Judge would go silent and then 'exit in haste'.

Some of the excuses offered by the various Clerks or Registrars afterwards were:

"The Judge clearly said, "Any other business?" (He must have mumbled because somehow we didn't hear that).

"Once the Judge rises, he cannot continue business." (This is clearly NOT true - or at least, is not a consistent rule).

"You didn't tell us in advance that you were going to make these applications." (We don't need to. But even when we DID tell the Courts Service in advance, they came up with some other excuse not to go ahead).

D. Gardaí blocking access to the Court. Again, another unconstitutional act. On this occasion in Castlebar, Gardaí would only allow ONE person at a time inside to have their case heard, and only those people who were already 'on the list'. Those of us with Common Informer applications were simply blocked from going in. This is absolutely unlawful.

E. Judges declaring the paperwork 'not in order'. This ploy has also been tried a few times and is usually another ruse because first of all it is very hard to get the simple C. I. forms 'wrong'. Secondly, some judges have readily accepted forms that other judges have declared 'not in order' - so you can't rely on judicial consistency here either. In any event, you can simply ask the judge to explain what is wrong (because you are only a simple member of the public) and the judge is duty-bound to give you some latitude.

F. Judges saying they 'need time' to consider the paperwork. Usually this is nonsense, as the whole premise behind the Common Informer process is that you go before a Judge with *proof* that a crime has been committed. So unless you have a lengthy statement or complicated evidence, you should respectfully insist that the judge deals with the application there-and-then, because once the judge leaves the Courtroom with (or without) your applications, any number of 'complications' or delays may arise that could stop the matter going forwards.

G. Judges trying to make a summary offence 'indictable'. The reason they want to do this is because jurisdiction is then handed over to the DPP's Office - and YOU lose control of the process.

H. Judges telling us that there has been a lengthy Supreme Court ruling which they will have to consult beforehand. On that occasion, the judge then slipped out of the Courtroom despite all the paperwork being in order. So we went ahead and read that Supreme Court ruling and discovered that it absolutely supports and reinforces our right to private prosecutions. (See p. 40)

I. Court Clerks scribbling notes and handing us back our paperwork. Do not accept this. Hand the forms straight back to them, along with the 'Personal Declaration' (if you haven't already done so) which advises them about the dangers of NOT following due process.

Whatever trick or ploy is used to try to obstruct or delay you, just remember that anyone working in our justice system simply cannot argue with the Supreme Court findings of July 2015 - nor can they go against precedent or current legislation. These findings are absolutely binding - and especially on more junior Judges and/or Courts - because our legal system is based on three main principles: **(i) Judicial precedent** (case history and previous decisions); **(ii) Legislation** (current acts, laws and statutes); and **(iii) Supreme Court Rulings** (which basically trump the other two). And the good news for us is that all three of these spheres absolutely support and reinforce the right of private prosecution under the Common Informer legislation.

The D.I.Y. Common Informer Procedure

The unearthing of a process long enshrined in Common Law whereby an ordinary citizen can apply directly to the District Court for a summons in order to hold another citizen to account for alleged wrongs, has been a most welcome discovery. However, despite this process being robustly defended by no less a figure than Justice Gerald Hogan in 2013 as well as the Supreme Court in 2015, and despite all the quotes in our Constitution about 'equal justice for all' - it seems that the establishment - or at least those elements of the establishment who would prefer to remain unaccountable for their errant actions - are determined to obstruct or forestall any attempts by the public to avail of this legislation. Here's hoping that the information on the following pages will help ordinary citizens avail of justice without the necessity of having to rely on 'the authorities' or on costly legal teams to secure *some* accountability on the part of those who believe they are above the law.

The following pages detail the Court Rules and the respective legislation involved. As usual, the legal verbiage is unnecessarily obtuse, complicated and difficult to wade through, and you can be absolutely sure that if you make even the slightest error in 'procedure' the establishment will leap at that chance to prevent your prosecution going forwards. This has already been demonstrated in various Courthouses around the country where some of the most outrageous incidents of overt bias, injustice, breaches of due process, collusion between State agencies, and assaults and intimidation by Gardaí, have been deployed against lay litigants who have attempted to enforce this legislation.

But don't be disheartened, because with each and every illegitimate attempt by the authorities to prevent or forestall these legitimate prosecutions going forwards brings thousands more eyes to bear on what is *really* going on in our Courts and in the corridors of power in Ireland today.

The Common Informer Procedure
& Things To Watch Out For!

1. First of all, make sure you have an absolutely solid case to present, with clear and unequivocal evidence of a wrong having been committed against you. You should be asking yourself; do I have the proof? Do I have eye witnesses?

2. Identify the specific crime(s) that have been committed and whichever Acts, Laws or Statutes have been breached. A simple google search on *http://www.irishstatutebook.ie/* or the lists in the *I-I SOS Guide* will help here.

3. Decide whether you are going for 'summary' or 'indictable' charges, and prepare to follow through. Don't forget that 'indictable' charges will be taken over by the DPP's Office - who may - or may not prosecute the alleged offender. If the offender works for the State, then the chances of them being prosecuted on indictment drops dramatically.

4. Decide which District Court you need to approach. You may have to seek clarity from the Courts Service (or a solicitor) on this point depending on;

   (i) where the offence was committed;

   (ii) by whom; and/or

   (iii) where the crime was reported, and

   (iv) whether or not you can use a Court in your own jurisdiction, or, in the offender's jurisdiction.

The general rule however is that your local Court is definitely the place to start. But please be careful of 'tipping your hand' when making enquiries of the Courts Service or of solicitors because our experience so far is that they may collude with the accused (in one form or another) to try to obstruct the process going forwards.

These are the District Court Rules regarding jurisdiction for criminal offences as per **Amendment to: Order 13, S.I. No. 41 of 2008: District Court (Criminal Justice Act 2007)**

Criminal proceedings shall be brought, heard and determined—

(a)   in the court area wherein the offence charged or, if more than one offence is stated to have been committed within a Judge's district, any one of such offences is stated to have been committed; or

(b)   in criminal cases where no offence has been charged, in the court area wherein the offence is stated to have been committed; or

(c)   in the court area wherein the accused has been arrested; or

(d)   in the court area wherein the accused resides; or

(e)   in the court area specified by order made pursuant to the provisions of section 15 of the Courts Act 1971; or

(f)   in a case to which section 79A(1) of the Courts of Justice Act 1924 (inserted by section 178 of the Criminal Justice Act 2006) applies, in any court area within any of the districts referred to in that subsection, or

(g)   in the case of proceedings under any provision of the Companies Acts referred to in section 240A of the Companies Act 1963 against a company or an officer of a company, in the court area in which the registered office of the company is situated or in any other court area permitted by that section.

5. According to the official 1851 rules you now have a choice to either; (a) walk straight into a District Court hearing and *verbally* address the Judge and make your

allegations; or (b) you fill out the appropriate forms (15.3 & 15.1) and present them to the Court. You can also add a separate sworn statement if you cannot fit all the details on Form 15.3. Those who have tried the purely verbal approach report that Judges insisted they had to use Forms 15.3 & 15.1 - so we will continue with that process here. However, there is an obvious case for anyone with a learning disability (for example) to commence the application verbally and let the Court issue directions thereafter. One would imagine that the Court is obliged to facilitate anyone who cannot complete the paperwork 'in the overall interests of justice'.

6. Print out **Form 15.3 Information** (from p. 87) or, go to your local Courts Service Office and *try* to get copies. (Reports coming in indicate that the Courts Service has not been very forthcoming of late). You can also download them from the Courts Service website or simply Google *"Form 15.3"*. There is NO charge for these forms, and NO duty to be paid - so please do not let them convince you otherwise. In fact, if they try to delay or obstruct you in any way, or try to charge you money for the forms or the summons, then warn them that they going against 165 years of precedent, against Common Law and recent Superior Court rulings and therefore may be 'interfering in the administration of justice'.

7. Fill out the information form (15.3) in clear language, making sure all of the required details are included. Although the legislation clearly states that we only need to make the allegation "in common language" our experience so far is that the Judge will try to declare the paperwork 'unacceptable' if you haven't listed the specific crimes committed - and which Law, Act or Statute has been broken. (Please see Irish Statute Book website for that list)

8. Fill out as much detail as you can on the **Summons Form 15.1** (on p. 88) likewise, and make sufficient copies of both forms to be lodged with the Court, served on the other party or parties, and to keep for yourself.

9. Take the forms into the next sitting of the District Court and present them directly to the Clerk, Registrar or Judge along with one of the statements on pages 84 and 86. Obviously, presenting the Court with what is in effect a warning statement that advises the 'Officers of the Court' that they have to follow due process might well irritate them - but on the other hand, it makes it clear to the Court that you will not stand for any nonsense or delays. Please note that the Courts Service have advised us that for practical reasons they would *prefer* if we notified them in advance of any intention to request a summons from a Judge, but apparently this is NOT explicitly required by the rules. You will have to weigh up the advantages and disadvantages of extending a courtesy that might work against your interests if the Court Service has advance notice of your intentions.

10. Having delivered the paperwork into the hands of the Clerk, take a seat and wait for your application to be called. Be prepared to wait to the end of the day's business if necessary, because first of all you have delivered your paperwork at the last minute, and secondly, because another tactic being used to frustrate us is to wait until everyone else has departed (so there are no witnesses) and then the Judge suddenly 'exits in haste' or produces some convoluted excuse to stall us. Another ploy is to hear our applications just before lunch - or, after everyone else has gone to lunch - again, so there are fewer witnesses to any shenanigans. So please be alert to any signal that the Judge is preparing to rise or leave, and make sure you get their attention before they exit the Courtroom. In any event, as long as the Clerk has accepted your paperwork, then the matter MUST be heard... so please don't accept any excuses otherwise.

11. The Judge will then ask you about the offence and the evidence and if all is in order should then sign the summons. However, in order to forestall any last-ditch efforts by the opposition to block your prosecution going forwards after-the-fact (such as taking judicial review proceedings based

on the District Court Judge *not* doing his job properly) please make sure that you question the Judge 'on the record' as to whether all the procedures and protocols have been properly followed - and then thank the Judge for his/her service.

12. Next, you 'serve' the summons on the accused either in person or by pre-paid registered post. Make sure you are absolutely clear on what the service requirements are, or else this will afford the opposition another opportunity to obstruct the progress of the case - or even dismiss it altogether - as has already happened. There are the District Court Rules:

> *(a) by sending, by registered prepaid post, a copy thereof in an envelope addressed to him at his last known residence or most usual place of abode or at his place of business in the State,*

> *(b) by sending, by any other system of recorded delivery prepaid post specified in rules of court, a copy thereof in such an envelope as aforesaid, or*

> *(c) by delivery by hand, by a person other than the person on whose behalf it purports to be issued authorised in that behalf by rules of court, of a copy thereof in such an envelope as aforesaid.*

13. Once the summons has been 'served' on the opposition, then you need to return to the Court Office and lodge your proof of service and a copy of the served summons with them - at least four days before the hearing date.

Order 10, District Court Rules, S.I. No. 285 of 2012 -

Time for service and lodgment of documents

> *21. Save where otherwise provided by statute or by these Rules, a document which is required to be served shall be served at least seven days or, in the case of service by registered prepaid post, at least 21 days, before the date fixed for the hearing.*

22. A document intended for entry for hearing shall, together with a statutory declaration as to service thereof, be lodged with the Clerk at least four days before the date fixed for the hearing.

23. No document shall be received or entered by the Clerk after the time specified by these Rules without the order of the Judge, and any late entry shall be made in accordance with such direction as the Judge may give.

14. Turn up in Court on the appointed day to assume the role of prosecutor. Make sure you are well prepared with a clear and progressive list of questions, and that you have all of your evidence and witnesses to hand. Do *not* think that you can simply 'wing it' and rely on verbal arguments and common sense, because you can be sure that the opposition *will* be well prepared and will be doing their utmost to undermine you - either within - or outside of the rules.

15. Naturally, you should ensure you are accompanied by other I-I members and that contemporaneous notes are taken during the hearing. Follow all the usual I-I procedures for attending Court (including wearing your I-I badges).

- Open with a Constitutional affirmation. (See p. 81)

- Ask for permission to record the proceedings due to so many instances of unreliable records issuing from the Courts. (You will be refused - but at least it's on the record)

- Confirm that the D.A.R. is on (digital audio recording) and advise the Court you will be seeking a copy.

- Ask all officials present to identify themselves and affirm their oaths of office.

- Make sure someone fills out a Court Hearing Report form (or similar) for your own records.

- Ask the Judge to guarantee your safety; that you will NOT be manhandled or assaulted by Gardaí as long as you behave in a lawful and respectful manner.

- Make sure that things progress at YOUR pace and with YOUR full understanding.

- Do not allow yourself to be intimidated, rushed, bamboozled, diverted or otherwise distracted from the matter at hand. Stay on script, politely but firmly.

- If the opposition does not abide by the rules, point this out 'for the record'.

- If the Judge does not abide by the rules - point this out 'for the record'- reminding the Court that you are 'standing by the Constitution' and you are requiring him/her to do the same.

- If there is any blatant disregard for the law, for Court Rules or for the Constitution, then have the courage to denounce the proceedings (politely but firmly) and read out your 'Constitutional Declaration of Non-Cooperation' (on p. 80) and exit the Courtroom.

- Then, <u>without delay</u>, lodge further Common Informer proceedings *and* criminal complaints with the Gardaí as against any and all who participated in the illegalities, including any Officers of the Court (clerks ' registrars / solicitors / barristers) and/or members of the judiciary. Send each a Formal Notification of a Criminal Complaint - and send a copy to *Integrity Ireland* for our records, and for publication.

Remember, it is crucially important that we follow up on each and every instance of wrongdoing because this will inspire others to take a stand whilst making it clear to rogue authority figures that official wrongdoing now comes at a personal cost - only this time, to them!

The original legislation dates back to the middle ages. It was given statutory form in Common Law in 1851 and is still in force today. However, given that this statute was formally introduced during British rule, any references to Britain or its other colonies; to out-of-date currency; or any other irrelevant reference, can of course be ignored.

There have of course been various changes to the law since this legislation was first drafted, most notably *Section 9(1) of the Criminal Justice (Administration) Act 1924* which abolished the right of Common Informers to *prosecute* cases on indictment (but we can still *initiate* indictable offences) but it will no doubt be helpful to understand the original procedures in context of 1851 Ireland, and the original intent and purpose for this important legislation which, to put it plainly, was to furnish direct access to justice for those who could ill afford a lawyer; or, for those occasions where the authorities failed (for one reason or another) to prosecute 'in the name of the people'; as well as to facilitate the initiation of criminal prosecutions based on the information provided and the considered decision of a single judge or magistrate.

It is important to note that if there have been no specific written amendments to the original clauses and sections, then those parts still remain as active law today.

*   *   *

PETTY SESSIONS (Ireland) ACT, 1851

Informations and Complaints.

10. Whenever information shall be given to any justice that any person has committed or is suspected to have committed any treason, felony, misdemeanor, or other offence, within the limits of the jurisdiction of such justice, for which such person shall be punishable either by indictment or upon a summary conviction; or that any person has committed or is suspected to have committed any such crime or offence elsewhere out of the jurisdiction

of such justice, either in Great Britain or Ireland, or in the Isles of Man, Jersey, Guernsey, Alderney, or Sark, and such person is residing or being, or is suspected to reside or be, within the limits of the jurisdiction of such justice; or that any person has committed or is suspected to have committed any crime or offence whatsoever on the high seas, or in any creek, harbour, haven, or other place in which the Admiralty of England or Ireland have or claim to have jurisdiction, or on land beyond the seas, for which an indictment can be legally preferred in any place in the United Kingdom of England and Ireland, and such person is residing or being, or is suspected to reside or be, within the limits of the jurisdiction of such justice; or whenever a complaint shall be made to any justice as to any other matter arising within the limits of his jurisdiction, upon which he shall have power to make a summary order, it shall be lawful for such justice to receive such information or complaint, and to proceed in respect to the same, subject to the following provisions:

1. Whenever it is intended that a summons only shall issue to require the attendance of any person, the information or complaint may be made either with or without oath, and either in writing or not, according as the justice shall see fit:

2. But whenever it is intended that a warrant shall issue for the arrest or committal of any person, the information or complaint shall be in writing, and on the oath of the complainant or of some person or persons, on his behalf:

3. Whenever any such information shall have been taken on oath and in writing that any person has committed or is suspected to have committed any indictable crime or offence (or any offence for which such person shall be punishable upon summary

58

conviction, and for whose arrest the justice shall issue a warrant), it shall be lawful for the justice, if he shall see fit, to bind the informant or complainant by recognizance (A a.*) or (C.) to appear at the court or place where the defendant is to be tried or the complaint is to be heard to prosecute or give evidence, as the case may be, against such person:

4. In all cases of summary jurisdiction the complaint shall be made, when it shall relate to the nonpayment of any poor rate, county rate, or other public tax, at any time after the date of the warrant authorizing the collection of the same, and, when it shall relate to the nonpayment of money for wages, hire, or tuition, within one year from the termination of the term or period in respect of which it shall be payable, and, when it shall relate to any trespass, within two months from the time when the trespass shall have occurred, and in any other case within six months from the time when the cause of complaint shall have arisen, but not otherwise:

And in all cases of summary jurisdiction any person against whom any such information or complaint shall have been made in writing shall, upon being amenable or appearing in person or by counsel or attorney, be entitled to receive from the clerk of petty sessions a copy of such information or complaint, on payment of the sum of sixpence to such clerk; and such clerk shall in no case allow the original information or complaint to be taken out of his possession.

Process to enforce appearance.
11. The manner in which persons against whom any such informations or complaints as aforesaid shall have been received by any justice shall be made to appear to answer to the same shall be subject to the following provisions:

1. In all cases of indictable crimes and offences (where an information that any person has committed the same shall have been taken in writing and on oath) the justice shall issue a warrant (B b.) to arrest and bring such person before him, or some other justice of the same county, to answer to the complaint made in the information (and which warrant may be issued or executed on a Sunday as well as on any other day); or if he shall think that the ends of justice would be thereby sufficiently answered, it shall be lawful for him, instead of issuing such warrant, to issue a summons in the first instance to such person, requiring him to appear and answer to the said complaint; but nothing herein contained shall prevent any justice from issuing a warrant for the arrest of such person at any time before or after the time mentioned in such summons for his appearance; and whenever such person shall afterwards appear or be brought before any such justice, he shall proceed according to the provisions herein-after contained as to taking the evidence against such person, and committing such person for trial:

2. In all cases of summary jurisdiction the justice may issue his summons (B a.) directed to such person, requiring him to appear and answer to the complaint; and it shall not be necessary that such justice shall be the justice or one of the justices by whom the complaint shall be afterwards heard and determined; and in all cases of offences where such person shall not appear at the required time and place, and it shall be proved on oath either that he was personally served with such summons or that he is keeping out of the way of such service, (the complaint being in writing and on oath,) the justice may issue a warrant to arrest and bring such person before him or some other justice of the same county, to answer to the said complaint;

and when such person shall afterwards be arrested under such warrant, the justice before whom he shall be brought may either by warrant (E b.) commit him to gaol, until the hearing of the complaint, or may discharge him upon his entering into a recognizance (C), with or without sureties, at the discretion of the justice, conditioned for his appearance at such hearing:

And each summons or warrant shall be signed by the justice or one of the justices issuing the same, and it shall state shortly the cause of complaint, and no summons or warrant shall be signed in blank; and in every case where the offence shall have occurred or the cause of complaint shall have arisen within the petty sessions district for which the justice issuing any such summons or warrant shall act, but the party or witness to whom such summons shall be directed or against whom such warrant shall be issued shall reside in an adjoining county, it shall be lawful for such justice to compel the appearance of such party or witness at the hearing of the charge or complaint within such district, in like manner as if such party or witness resided in such district, although such justice may not be a justice of such adjoining county.

Service of summonses. (*Abridged*)
3. Every summons shall be served upon the person to whom it is directed by delivering to him a copy of such summons, or, if he cannot be conveniently met with, by leaving such copy for him at his last or most usual place of abode, or at his office, warehouse, counting-house, shop, factory, or place of business, with some inmate of the house not being under sixteen years of age, a reasonable time before the hearing of the complaint; and such last-mentioned service shall be deemed sufficient service of such summons in every case except where personal service shall be specially required by this Act; and in every case the person who shall serve such summons shall

endorse on the same the time and place where it was served, and shall attend with the same at the hearing of the complaint to depose., if necessary, to such service:

Powers to enforce attendance of witnesses.

13. Whenever it shall be made to appear to any justice that any person within the jurisdiction of such justice is able to give material evidence for the prosecution in cases of indictable offences, or for the complainant or defendant in cases of summary jurisdiction, and will not voluntarily appear for the purpose of being examined as a witness, such justice may proceed as follows:

1. He may issue a summons (B a.) to such person, requiring him to appear at a time and place mentioned in such summons, to testify what he may know concerning the matter of the information or complaint, and (if the justice shall see fit) to bring with him and produce for examination such accounts, papers, or other documents, as shall be in his possession or power, and as shall be deemed necessary by such justice; but in any case of an indictable crime or offence, whenever the justice shall be satisfied by proof upon oath that it is probable that such person will not attend to give evidence without being compelled so to do, then, (the information or complaint being in writing and on oath,) instead of issuing such summons as aforesaid, he may issue a warrant (B b.) in the first instance for the arrest of such person:

2. And in any case, when any person to whom a summons shall be issued in the first instance shall neglect or refuse to appear at the time and place appointed by such summons, and no just excuse shall be offered for such neglect or refusal, then, (the information or complaint being in writing and on oath,) after proof upon oath that such summons was

personally served upon such person, or that such person is keeping out of the way of such service, and that he is able to give material evidence in the case, the justice before whom such person should have appeared may issue a warrant (B b.) to arrest such person, and to bring him at the time and place appointed for the hearing of the case, to testify and to produce such accounts, papers, and documents as may be required as aforesaid:

3. In all cases of prosecutions for offences the evidence of the informer or party aggrieved shall be admissible in proof of the offence; and in all cases of complaints on which a justice can make an order for the payment of money, or otherwise, the evidence of the complainant shall be admissible in proof of his complaint; and in cases of wages, hire, or tuition the evidence of the master or employer may, in the discretion of the justices, be admitted in proof against the complaint:

4. All witnesses shall be examined upon oath; and any justice before whom any such witness shall appear for the purpose of being so examined shall have full authority to administer to every such witness the usual oath.

5. Whenever any person shall appear as a witness, either in obedience to a summons or by virtue of a warrant, (or shall be present, and shall be verbally required by the justice or justices to give evidence,) and he shall refuse to be examined upon oath concerning the matter of the information or complaint, or shall refuse to take such oath, or having taken such oath shall refuse to answer such questions concerning the said matter as shall then be put to him, or shall refuse or neglect to produce any such accounts, papers, or documents as aforesaid, (without, offering any just

excuse for such refusal,) the justice or justices then present may adjourn the proceedings for any period not exceeding eight clear days, and may in the meantime by warrant (E b.) commit the said witness to gaol, unless he shall sooner consent to be sworn or to testify as aforesaid, or to produce such accounts, papers, or documents, as the case may be; and if such witness, upon being brought up upon such adjourned hearing, shall again refuse to be sworn, or to testify as aforesaid, or to produce such accounts, papers, or documents, as the case may be, the said justices, If they shall see fit, may again adjourn the proceedings, and commit the witness for the like period, and so again from time to time until he shall consent to be sworn or to testify as aforesaid, or to produce such accounts, papers, or documents, as the case may be (provided that no such imprisonment shall in any case of summary jurisdiction exceed one month in the whole); but nothing herein contained shall be deemed to prevent the justice or justices from sending any such case for trial, or otherwise disposing of the same in the meantime, according to any other sufficient evidence which shall have been received by him or them:

6. Whenever in cases of indictable offences the justice or justices shall see fit, they may bind the witnesses by recognizance (A b.*) or (C.) to appear at the trial of the offender and give evidence against him; and whenever any witness shall refuse to be so bound it shall be lawful for the justice or justices by warrant (E b.) to commit him to the gaol of the county or place in which the person accused is to be tried, there to be imprisoned until the trial of the person accused, unless in the meantime such witness shall duly enter into recognizance (C.) before some justice of the county in which such gaol shall be situated; but if afterwards, from want of sufficient evidence or other cause, the

justice or justices before whom the person accused shall have been brought shall not commit him or hold him to bail, it shall be lawful for such justice or justices or any other justice of the county by warrant (E d.) to order the keeper of the gaol to discharge such witness:

7. In all cases of summary jurisdiction it shall be lawful for the justices by whom any order for payment of money, not being in the nature of a penalty for an offence, shall be made, to order the party at whose instance any witness shall have been summoned to pay to such witness such sum, not exceeding two shillings and sixpence, as to such justices shall seem fit, for his expenses or loss of time for each day of attending to give evidence, and, in default of payment thereof at such time as such justice shall appoint, then to issue a, warrant to levy the amount thereof by distress of the goods of such party:

And no person who shall be summoned to attend before any court of petty sessions, or before any justice out of petty sessions, as a witness, shall be liable to arrest for debt whilst at such court, or at the place where such justice shall sit, or whilst proceeding to or returning from the same, provided he shall proceed and return by the most direct road without unnecessary delay; and it shall be lawful for the court out of which the writ or process shall have issued to order the discharge of any person who shall be so arrested.

Court Rules Pertaining to the Common Informer Procedure

1. (1). Where in the first instance a summons is sought pursuant to section 10 of the Petty Sessions (Ireland) Act 1851 to require the attendance before the Court of a person against whom a complaint is made, the complaint shall be made to a Judge and may be made with or without oath as the Judge shall direct.

(2). Where the complaint is made on oath it shall be made by sworn information (Form 15.3 Schedule B).

(3). Having received such complaint, the Judge may issue a summons (Form 15.1 Schedule B) in any case in which that Judge has jurisdiction in the district to which he or she is assigned.

Application to and issue of summons by Court Office.
2. (1). When, upon application made to an appropriate office (within the meaning of section 1(14) of the Courts (No. 3) Act 1986 as amended) pursuant to section 1(3) of the Courts (No. 3) Act 1986 as amended, for the issue of a summons in relation to an offence, a summons is issued, such summons shall be in the Form 15.2 Schedule B.

Contents of summons and Court to which returnable.
3. (1). A summons shall state shortly and in ordinary language particulars of the cause of complaint or offence alleged, and shall state the name of the person against whom the complaint has been made or who is alleged to have committed the offence and the address (if known) at which he or she ordinarily resides.

(2). A summons issued by an appropriate office and to which rule 2(1) of this Order relates shall also notify such person that he or she will be accused of that offence at a sitting of the District Court to be specified in the summons. Such summons shall also contain the particulars specified in section 1(6) of the Courts (No. 3) Act 1986 as amended.

(3). Every summons shall require the appearance of the person to whom it is directed at a sitting of the Court having jurisdiction to deal with the complaint or the offence alleged, provided that the court at which such person is required to appear shall -

> (a) Where the summons is issued by a Judge, be a court within the area of jurisdiction, of that Judge, or

> (b) Where the summons is issued by an appropriate office be a court within the district in which a judge has jurisdiction in relation to the offence to which the summons relates.

4.   Two or more complaints or offences may be alleged in the one summons.

O.15, r.5 Signing of summonses
5.   (1). A summons issued by a Judge shall be signed by the Judge who issues it and no summons shall be signed in blank.

(2). A summons against a person who is a member of the Garda Síochána shall be signed by a Judge.

(3). (a) Where a summons is signed by a Judge such summons shall not be avoided by reason of the death of that Judge or by reason of his or her ceasing to hold office

> (b) Where a summons is issued by an appropriate office such summons shall not be avoided by reason of the death of the appropriate District Court Clerk whose name is specified on the summons or by reason of his or her ceasing to hold office.

Copies for service

6.   In the case of every summons issued otherwise than by transmitting it by electronic means to the person who applied for it or a person acting on his or her behalf, there shall be issued with such summons a copy thereof for service upon each person to whom the summons is directed. Where a summons is issued by transmitting it by electronic means to the person who applied for it or a person acting on his or her behalf, a true copy of such summons shall be served upon each person to whom the summons is directed by electronic means.

May be served in any part of the State.

7.   A summons may be served in any part of the State and upon service being effected in a manner prescribed by these Rules, the person against whom the complaint is made or the offence is alleged shall be as effectively bound by the proceedings as if he or she resided within the area of jurisdiction of the Judge issuing it or (if issued out of an appropriate office) within the limits of the court area or areas to which the appropriate Clerk whose name is specified on the summons has been assigned.

8.   Where an enactment constituting an offence states the offence to be the doing or the omission to do any one of a number of different acts in the alternative, or states any part of the offence in the alternative, the acts, omissions or other matters stated in the alternative in the enactment may be stated either in the alternative or in the conjunctive in the summons alleging such offence.

9.   In alleging an offence contrary to any statute or statutes it shall be sufficient to state the substance of the offence in ordinary language with such particulars of the offence as may be necessary for giving reasonable information as to the nature of the complaint, and it shall not be necessary to negative any exception or exemption from or qualification to the operation of a statute creating such offence.

Summons in lieu of a warrant

10. Where under Order 16, rule 1(1) of these Rules a warrant is sought for the arrest of a person charging that person with having committed an indictable offence a Judge may, if he or she thinks fit, instead of issuing a warrant issue a summons requiring the appearance of that person, notwithstanding that the complaint had been made by information on oath and in writing. A Judge who has issued such summons may at any time (the complaint having been made by information) issue a warrant for the arrest of that person.

Sketches courtesy of www.maggieblanck.com)

---

* Provisions relating to the issue of summonses in matters other than criminal matters are contained in Order 99 of these Rules. (See following)

District Court Rules, Order: 99

Issue of summonses by a clerk in matters other than criminal matters *

[Summons — application for]
1.   Whenever it is intended to commence proceedings (not being proceedings to which the Courts (No. 3) Act, 1986 relates) in the District Court against a person, and the issue of a summons is sought requiring the appearance of that person before the Court, on a matter or issue which the Court has jurisdiction to hear and determine, application to sign and issue such summons may, unless otherwise provided, be made to the Clerk for the court area wherein that person ordinarily resides or carries on any profession, business or occupation.

[— Form of, signing and issue of]
2.   The applicant for the issue of such summons shall lodge with such Clerk a duly completed summons in the Form 99.1, Schedule C (or such modification thereof as may be appropriate), together with a copy or copies for service. The Clerk shall unless otherwise provided by statute or by rules of court, list the matter or issue for hearing at a sitting of the Court, record the place, date and time of hearing on each document and, having signed and dated the same, shall issue them to the applicant for service.

[— Court to which returnable]
3.   Every summons issued under this Order shall require the appearance of each person to whom it is directed at a sitting of the Court having jurisdiction to deal with the matter or issue set out in the summons, provided that such sitting shall be a sitting of the Court for the court area to which such Clerk is assigned and shall be within the district in which a Judge of the District Court has jurisdiction in relation to the matter or issue aforesaid.

[— Service of lodgment of]
4. Save where otherwise provided, the provisions of Order 10 (Service of Documents) of these Rules shall mutatis mutandis apply to summonses signed and issued in proceedings to which this Order relates.

[— Order 15 (in part) to apply to]
5. The provisions of rules 4, 5, 6, 7, 8 and 9 (with any necessary modifications) of Order 15 of these Rules shall apply to summonses signed and issued in proceedings to which this Order relates.

---

*Provisions relating to the issue of summonses in respect of offences are contained in Order 15 of these Rules. (See previous pages)

"Prosecute a Banker"
(A DIY guide for Village readers)

The following article was written for Village Magazine in January, 2011 by Barrister Gary Fitzgerald kindly reproduced here with the advisory that its contents may not be precisely pertinent in Ireland's 2016 legal system, noting that 'the establishment' is, apparently, actively seeking ways to 'water down' the legislation precisely because of the potential to hold errant establishment figures to account. So, no great surprises there either! So, let's make use of this valuable piece of legislation while we still can.

Since the beginning of the banking crisis in September 2008, the government's strategy has been to protect the banks at all costs. With the IMF/EU deal announced recently, it is now clear that the government intends that the taxpayer will pay for bank losses irrespective of the impact on public services and on the wider economy. The final cost of this policy is not yet known, and it may never be known. We have lost track of the billions of euro already spent and the billions more promised. The government's decisions may lead to national bankruptcy. The voters will get a chance to express their opinion on this policy in the upcoming general election.

It is also clear that there will not be any criminal prosecution of senior bankers under this government. More than two years have passed since this crisis began and apart from a little grandstanding by the Gardaí in March 2010 (with the arrest of Sean FitzPatrick) and the occasional public statement by the Gardaí, nothing appears to have happened. In a previous article I wrote about how some of these criminal offences were not very complex. Two in particular carry jail terms of up to 5 years and a number of board members from both Anglo Irish Bank and Irish Life and Permanent could be prosecuted and face jail terms of up to 35 years. Voters may take direct action against politicians on polling day, but is there any direct action they may take to prosecute white-collar criminals?

The general rule in criminal law is that the State prosecutes the defendant on behalf of the people. For serious cases the Director of Public Prosecutions (DPP) initiates the prosecution and for minor offences it is the responsibility of the individual Garda who is in charge of the case to initiate a prosecution. But audit is not the only possible source of criminality that could ground an action; and the Financial Regulator is, for example, investigating allegations that banks provided "false and misleading information" to NAMA about the value of their toxic property loans.

But there is a little-used process whereby any individual may initiate a criminal prosecution. This is known as the right of Common Informer. Over recent years the rights of the Common Informer have been limited by Acts of the Oireachtas, but the basic right still exists. The rest of this article will set out the process involved in taking a criminal case by way of Common Informer. But first, it is necessary to explain some principles of sentencing in criminal law.

Sentencing Offenders
A summary offence is a minor offence, triable in the District Court, with the judge acting as both judge and jury. The maximum penalty is two years in jail or a fine of up to €5,000. An indictable offence is a serious offence, triable in the Circuit Criminal Court or the Central Criminal Court. The case is heard by a judge and jury and there is no limit on jail term or fine. The punishment available for any individual offence is set out in the relevant statute. For many crimes the statute sets out a punishment if the case is tried in the District Court and a heavier punishment if the case is heard in the Circuit Criminal Court. The choice of court is, in general, determined by the prosecuting authority (such as the DPP).

For example, S197 of the Companies Act 1990 makes it an offence for an officer of a company to give a false statement to the company's auditors. S240 (as amended) sets the punishment for that offence as follows:

Summary offence a fine of €1,900 and/or up to 1 year in jail

Indictable offence a fine of €12,600 and/or up to 5 years in jail

Should more than one false statement be given to auditors, for example, were a false statement made in each of 7 different years, the defendant could be charged with 7 instances of the same offence. Were the prosecution to be successful, it would be up to the judge to determine if the sentences should be served concurrently or consecutively. Were the former chosen then the defendant would serve a 5 year jail term, while in the latter case he would serve a 35 year jail term (5 years x 7 offences). The normal procedure is for concurrent sentences to be handed down but if the offences are serious enough then the judge may impose a consecutive sentence, or a combination of both.

The Common Informer procedure
Any private individual may initiate a criminal prosecution as a Common Informer. The process begins with the making of a complaint under S10 of the Petty Sessions Act 1851. That act states that a complaint is made to a judge of the District Court. If the judge is satisfied that there is a prima facia case then he must issue a summons for the defendant to appear in court to answer the complaint. The judge must ensure that there is substance to the complaint and may refuse to issue a summons. But the evidential threshold that the Common Informer must reach at this stage is low. There is no time-limit on the making of the complaint by the Common Informer for offences that may be tried either in the District Court or the Circuit Criminal Court.

Right at the outset the Common Informer has an important decision to make. He may seek a prosecution for summary offences only. In this case the Common Informer has full control of the prosecution and the DPP cannot interfere with the prosecution. Or the Common Informer may seek to try the offences as indictable offences. Here the Common Informer has control of the early stage of the proceedings but thereafter the DPP is obliged to take over. The DPP may either continue with the prosecution or decide to stop it.

This decision is a difficult one. On the one hand, in the District Court, the Common Informer has full control and there is no room for political interference. But on the other hand the possible punishment for the very serious crimes that have been committed is low. It may be that no one will ever spend time in jail for these banking offences due to inaction by the authorities. In this case, it would be a success if a 1 year jail term were handed down. Also the Common Informer must produce evidence to prove each element of the offence, a point which is discussed further below.

The solution here might be to initially seek to have the offences tried in the Circuit Criminal Court. If the DPP does not continue with the prosecution, then the case may be taken again, this time in the District Court. This should not fall foul of the long standing legal principle of double jeopardy. This states that it is not possible for a defendant to be tried for the same crime twice. It was developed as a vital protection of citizens from an abuse of the power of prosecution by the State. But according to S4A(4) of the Criminal Justice Act 1967 that does not arise in these circumstances.

If the DPP does not continue with the prosecution, another case may be taken at a later time. It is not clear if this section would withstand the inevitable constitutional challenge by any proposed defendants.

The Evidence

The most difficult part of any private criminal prosecution will be the gathering of evidence. The State has wide resources such as powers of arrest, search and seizure. It may detain suspects for questioning and ask the court to issue warrants for the searching of offices and private homes. The Common Informer has none of these resources, but the burden of proof is the same. In order for a prosecution to succeed, the Common Informer must be able to prove all the elements of the offence beyond a reasonable doubt. Attempting a prosecution without this evidence is, at best, counterproductive. Some of the white-collar crimes are complex, but others are relatively simple. But even for simple offences the evidence must be sufficient to meet the burden of proof. The offence of giving a misleading statement to an auditor contains the following elements:

- The statement must be false, misleading or deceptive;

- It must relate to a material fact;

- It must be made by an officer of the company;

- It must be made to the auditors of a company; and

- The defendant must have known the statement was false, or have made the statement recklessly.

The key evidence here would be the testimony of the auditors. The precise date and time of the making of the statement would need to be proven. Co-operation of the auditors would be desirable but not essential. Expert evidence must be tendered that proves that the misleading statement was material to the audit. Failure on any of those elements and the prosecution will also fail. But auditors are not the only possible crimes that could ground a and the Financial Regulator are investigating allegations that banks provided "false and misleading information" to NAMA about the value of their toxic property loans.

Conclusion

Following recent complaints from Michael McGrath TD, the Gardaí and the Financial Regulator are investigating allegations that banks provided "false and misleading information" to NAMA about the value of their toxic property loans. It is possible that complaints could also be made about possible inaccurate information provided by the banks some time before that – immediately before the bank guarantee. But both of these possible wrongdoings could also be prosecuted by Common Informers.

The right of a Common Informer is limited, but still very powerful. It has never been used in this way. Normally it is used as a procedural device to allow an individual Garda to initiate a prosecution. There is no reason why a properly researched, funded and proven case would not work. Any case would need to have access to legal advice from criminal lawyers, financial advice from accountants and auditors and sufficient resources to deal with the legal challenges that the powerful defendants would inevitably raise. But if the DPP and the incoming government fail to take action against Ireland's corporate criminals, ordinary citizens should use this residual power. It is vital for the future of our democracy that the rich and powerful are treated by the law on equal terms as the poor and weak.

Gary Fitzgerald is a practising barrister and recently resigned as chairman of the Greens National Executive Council.

Village Magazine, January 2011

*   *   *

So, no excuses any more folks - and no more whinging and moaning about what the bad guys have been up to.. because here's your golden opportunity to take the initiative. Stop being a soft target for tricksters, thugs, tyrants and thieves in the corridors of power. This is OUR country and OUR children's futures they are messing with. 100 years since the Rising - and nearly 70 years of supposed independence - and we are *still* being taken for fools and amadáns by a corrupt, arrogant, governing elite. 700 years of sweat, tears and bloodshed in order to throw off the yoke of oppression and injustice - and yet here we are all over again…?

As Chief Justice Susan Denham wrote;

> *"The driving concept of the Constitution is the sovereignty of the People and that all powers of government come from them.*
>
> *Article 40.3 of the Constitution has been interpreted by the Courts as protecting unenumerated rights which are not written in the constitutional text. The Constitution is interpreted by the judiciary as a living entity to reflect the contemporary times of the Irish People. It is a Living Constitution reflecting today's reality as much as that of 1937.*
>
> *In the Preamble of the Constitution the dignity of the person is a central concept and the right to human dignity is now a part of human rights law at an international and European level. Indeed, this very Irish concept of dignity is contained in 80 per cent of constitutions adopted since WWII.*
>
> *The centrality of dignity goes back to the Brehon Laws which made it an offence to shame a person, particularly those with a disability. This emphasises the long history and importance of dignity in Irish law and our heralding the concept to the world through our history, emigration and constitution."*

It seems that many in Government and in the employ of the State need to be urgently reminded of these fundamental facts!

Making A Citizen's Arrest

Another tactic being used by pro-justice groups is the option to place errant authority figures 'under arrest' because 'any person' may do so under certain circumstances. If for example a Garda, a civil servant or an Officer of the Court is engaged in an offence against the administration of justice, then that is the sort of indictable offence which qualifies us (i.e. 'any person') to make a citizen's arrest. But there are a couple of important things to watch out for.

Firstly, given that we don't have our own private Courts, jails or police forces; and given that we don't really want to be getting into physical confrontations which might lead to counter-charges of assault or kidnapping; and given we are required by the existing legislation to transfer custody to the Garda Síochána as soon as possible, then the first thing to understand is that these 'citizen's arrests' are purely verbal and largely symbolic. But this doesn't make them any less legitimate or any less powerful.

You see, we can *legitimately* state to the wrongdoer that they are committing an offence, and then ask them to surrender themselves into our custody - to be delivered to the nearest Garda Station for processing. Invariably they will refuse, look dumfounded and/or react violently, but no matter how they react, the fact remains that they HAVE been placed legitimately 'under arrest' and *someone* in authority now has to accept jurisdiction for those arrests.

Our tactic of late has been to write directly to the Garda Commissioner advising that certain Gardaí, Registrars and Judges (for example) have been placed under citizen's arrest - and will the Commissioner please accept jurisdiction? Their abject failure to do so places Garda Management in the uncomfortable position of; (i) failing to do their jobs, (ii) breaching legislation, and (iii) committing an additional offence against the administration of justice - which is an indictable offence subject to citizen's arrest.. etc, etc. ☺

Criminal Law Act, 1997

4.—(1) Subject to subsections (4) and (5), any person may arrest without warrant anyone who is or whom he or she, with reasonable cause, suspects to be in the act of committing an arrestable offence.

(2) Subject to subsections (4) and (5), where an arrestable offence has been committed, any person may arrest without warrant anyone who is or whom he or she, with reasonable cause, suspects to be guilty of the offence.

(3) Where a member of the Garda Síochána, with reasonable cause, suspects that an arrestable offence has been committed, he or she may arrest without warrant anyone whom the member, with reasonable cause, suspects to be guilty of the offence.

(4) An arrest other than by a member of the Garda Síochána may only be effected by a person under subsection (1) or (2) where he or she, with reasonable cause, suspects that the person to be arrested by him or her would otherwise attempt to avoid, or is avoiding, arrest by a member of the Garda Síochána.

(5) A person who is arrested pursuant to this section by a person other than a member of the Garda Síochána shall be transferred into the custody of the Garda Síochána as soon as practicable.

(6) This section shall not affect the operation of any enactment restricting the institution of proceedings for an offence or prejudice any power of arrest conferred by law apart from this section.

The key, as always, is to follow through with private criminal prosecutions each and every time you are wronged until 'they' finally get the message: *"Please - just do your jobs properly and respect the law and the Constitution!"*

For more information on making a citizen's arrest, please see P.148-152 of the *I-I SOS Guide* or the Wikipedia article.

CONSTITUTIONAL AFFIRMATION

This affirmation is respectfully made with due deference to this honourable Court, in the sincere anticipation of a fair and just outcome.

As a citizen of this country (and/or a member of the Irish public / the EU etc) I respectfully assert my right to fair, equitable and expedient treatment, as per the respective Articles of the Irish Constitution; the Judicial Code of Conduct; and the Charter of Fundamental Rights of the European Union.

I respectfully request that any and all incidences of fraud, perjury or manifest deception that arise during this hearing result in the appropriate response by the Court; that those responsible will be referred for criminal prosecution; that any such tainted evidence will be dismissed; and that the Court rigorously applies whatever financial penalties are due, including the rule of costs.

This affirmation is respectfully made with due deference to this honourable Court, in the sincere anticipation of a fair and just outcome.

CONSTITUTIONAL GROUNDS
FOR NON-COOPERATION

"The highest law in the State is the Constitution of Ireland, from which all other law derives its authority. The Constitution is held to be the source of power exercised by the legislative, judicial and executive branches of government. The Irish Supreme Court and High Court exercise judicial review over all legislation and may strike down laws if they are inconsistent with the constitution."

1. The Constitution supersedes the law. The law is subject to the Constitution.

2. Judges swear a solemn Constitutional Oath to abide by the law and the Constitution.

3. If a judge – or any other agent of the State is engaged in unlawful or unconstitutional activity – then they are NOT operating under their Constitutional or Statutory remits.

4. No citizen (or person) is obliged to facilitate or comply with illicit directions, procedures or processes. In fact, we are constitutionally and legally obliged NOT to knowingly do so.

5. To knowingly comply with, facilitate, or cooperate with unconstitutional activity is therefore to be complicit in criminal activity.

6. No other citizen – regardless of position – has the Constitutional right, nor the legal power, nor the moral authority to coerce, direct or manipulate another person into wrongdoing.

7. We therefore assert our fundamental right to refuse to be made knowingly complicit in illicit, under-handed or criminal activity on the basis of the Irish Constitution and the law.

In the matter before the Court today, the following facts are beyond dispute and collectively demonstrate that improper, illicit and/or illegal acts are being committed by parties to this case, and that said acts, and the resultant response or lack thereof by those entrusted with the administration of justice, clearly constitutes a collective attempt to pervert, interfere with or obstruct the course of justice, which is a criminal offence, and in clear breach of Articles 34, 35, 40 & 45 of the Constitution:

(You can list the specific reasons here below – or – use the statement above as a stand-alone declaration)

That to comply with such a process in these circumstances would be to sanction, or be complicit in unconstitutional or criminal activity, which the Respondent is NOT prepared to do.

Signed:

Personal Declaration to Accompany a Common Informer Application to the District Court

I _____ being of 18 years or older, of _____
_____
hereby submit to the Court this application for the issue of summonses as per the legislation outlined in the *Petty Sessions (Ireland) Act 1851*; as supported by the High Court ruling of July 9th 2013 and the Supreme Court ruling of July 30th 2015.

I wish it noted that I have supplied the 'Informations' on Form 15.3 "in common language" as required by legislation and precedent, and have accompanied the same with Form 15.1 for the issuance of a summons.

I respectfully draw the attention of the Court that according to Common Law, to current legislation, to long-standing precedent and to the aforesaid Superior Court rulings; that provided I have demonstrated *prima facie* evidence of the crime alleged, that this Court is obliged to issue said summons without further delay or prevarication, and I respectfully require that it does so.

I further note that the Courts Service has sent a comprehensive memo in 2015 to all District Court Judges advising them of the procedures and protocols to be followed, and that should there be any doubt or confusion on the part of this Court as to how to proceed, that I hold in my possession details of the aforesaid legislation, legal precedents and Superior Court rulings for the information of this Court – for the prompt and speedy advancement of this case.

In light of a number of previous 'difficulties' in advancing legitimate private prosecutions via the Irish District Courts, I regret I must respectfully advise this Court that in the event that any Officer of this Court attempts to improperly obstruct, delay, forestall or otherwise prevent this matter from advancing today; that any such action may be interpreted either/or as;

(i) a corrupt act, or misconduct in public office;

(ii) an act of conspiracy;

(iii) an attempt to pervert the course of justice, and/or

(iv) an attempt to interfere in the administration of justice,

Which are each criminal offences as against *S.1 of the Prevention of Corruption Act 1906*, and/or *S.41 of the Criminal Justice Act 1999, or S.71 of the Criminal Justice Act 2006* respectively, which will result in the appropriate action being taken according to law.

Signed

Date   Witness

Generic Statement to Accompany Your Common Informer Application to the District Court

I hereby submit to the Court this application for the issue of summonses as per the legislation outlined in the *Petty Sessions (Ireland) Act 1851*; as supported by the High Court ruling of July 9th 2013 and the Supreme Court ruling of July 30th 2016.

I wish it noted that I have supplied the 'Informations' on Form 15.3 "in common language" and have accompanied the same with Form 15.1 for the issuance of a summons.

I respectfully draw the attention of the Court to the fact that according to Common Law, to current legislation, to long-standing precedent and to the aforesaid Superior Court rulings; that provided I have demonstrated *prima facie* evidence of the crime alleged, that this Court is obliged to issue said summons without further delay or prevarication, and I respectfully require that it does so.

I further note that the Courts Service has sent a comprehensive memo in 2015 to all District Court Judges advising them of the procedures and protocols to be followed, and that should there be any doubt or confusion on the part of this Court as to how to proceed, that I hold in my possession details of the aforesaid legislation, legal precedents and Superior Court rulings for the information of this Court.

In the event that any Officer of this Court attempts to improperly obstruct, delay, forestall or otherwise prevent this matter from advancing today; that any such action may be interpreted as an attempt to pervert the course of justice, which is a criminal offence as against *S.7 of the Criminal Procedure Act 2010*, which will result in the appropriate action being taken according to law.

AN CHÚIRT DÚICHE   THE DISTRICT COURT

No. 15.3

O.15, r.1 (2)
O.16, r.1 (1)

Information

District Court Area of...District No................

.... Prosecutor

.... Accused

The information of ....

of...

who says on oath..

....

....

....

....

....

*(and the Informant binds himself/herself to attend when and where called on to give evidence against the said accused for the said offence, or otherwise to forfeit to the State the sum of...to the use of the Minister for Finance).

Signed..

Informant

Sworn before me this ....day of ....20.........

at...

Signed...
Judge of the District Court

* Delete where applicable

AN CHÚIRT DÚICHE   THE DISTRICT COURT

No. 15.1

O.15, r.1 (3)

Summons

District Court Area of..District No................

....*Complainant *Prosecutor

of...

....*Defendant *Accused

*(in court area and district aforesaid)

WHEREAS a complaint has been made to me that you, on the .... day of ....

20......., at .... *(in court area and district aforesaid)

did:...

....

....

....

....

THIS IS TO COMMAND YOU to appear on the hearing of the said complaint at a sitting of the
District Court for the court area and district aforesaid to be held at:

....on the ....day of ....20........

at....................*a.m. /p.m. to answer to the said complaint.

Dated this.......... day of ....20...........

Signed..
Judge of the District Court

To the above-named *defendant * accused...

of...

Delete where applicable

AN CHÚIRT DÚICHE   THE DISTRICT COURT

Schedule B
O.21, r.1 (1)

No. 21.1
Witness Summons

District Court Area of..District No...........

Prosecutor..

Accused...

YOU ARE HEREBY REQUIRED to attend at the sitting of the District Court to be held at

....on the ....day of .... 20...., at.......

*am/pm and on any day to which the hearing of these proceedings shall be adjourned, to give

evidence on behalf of .... on

the hearing of a complaint that the above-named accused did:...................................

....

....

....

*AND YOU ARE REQUIRED TO BRING WITH YOU the following accounts, papers, documents

(or things):...

....

....

Dated this...............day of.................................. 20........

Signed ....(Print name)...

* Judge of the District Court (or) Clerk of the District Court (or) Peace Commissioner

To..

Of...

**NOTE: If, without lawful excuse, you do not obey this summons, a warrant for your arrest
may be issued.**

*Delete where inapplicable

(Optional – for official stamp)

© Integrity Ireland 2015

89

"Legitimacy, Fairness and Credibility within the Criminal Justice System"

From the Irish Government White Paper on Crime, 2011

"In order to have ongoing public support and trust, criminal justice systems need to operate in a rule-based and accountable fashion. Arbitrary, corrupt or oppressive measures will ultimately undermine the authority and credibility of the system and, in turn, the rule of law generally. The Irish criminal justice system is founded on Constitutional and common law principles of fairness and respect for individual liberty, and, in particular, the right to a fair trial and a presumption of innocence. It is also essential, however, in the interests of efficiency and in order to instil public confidence, that the system functions effectively and protects the public.

Key overall components of a fair and credible system are:

• Effectiveness in detecting, deterring and punishing offending behaviour

• Fairness to all involved including victims, witnesses and accused

• Efficiency in the use of time and resources

• Transparency and prompt service delivery"

Are you listening Minister?

About the Author

Stephen Manning is a married father of three school-age children - one of whom has special needs. Stephen has worked in many occupations in several different countries, including the military (NATO), the haulage and building industries, sports & fitness instruction, adventure tourism, retail management, and more recently as a book publisher and a teacher of English in schools, colleges and universities both here and abroad. He holds a number of academic qualifications and diplomas in fields as diverse as sports medicine to the study of psychology and world religions. Stephen has also worked in various volunteer capacities as a sports instructor and official with Special Olympics, with the Y.M.C.A in the USA, and briefly with the Mayo Mountain Rescue Team. He is currently a part-time FAI registered referee with the Irish Soccer Referees Society.

Having returned to Ireland in 2005, Stephen found himself embroiled in a situation where he was obliged to issue civil proceedings against a 'politically connected' individual. It was the resulting traumatic experiences—including multiple serious failures of duty and assorted criminal acts by the statutory authorities—which eventually led to the setting up of the *Integrity Ireland* project in 2012.

Stephen is passionate about justice, and equally passionate about genuine democracy, which he believes is being lost to the unbridled ambitions of the connected elite.

Stephen ran as an independent candidate for Co. Mayo in the 2016 general election in order to highlight the aims and objectives of the *Integrity Ireland* project.

*   *   *

For more information or to book Stephen as a speaker please go to *CheckPoint Ireland* at www.checkpoint.ie

www.ingramcontent.com/pod-product-compliance
Lightning Source LLC
Chambersburg PA
CBHW060637210326
41520CB00010B/1637